TEAM OF ONE
Get the Sales Results of a Full Time Sales Team Without Actually Having One

David Traub

Copyright © 2014 David Traub

All rights reserved.

ISBN: 150238082X
ISBN-13: 978-1502380821

ALL RIGHTS RESERVED. This book contains material protected under International and Federal Copyright Laws and Treaties. Any unauthorized reprint or use of this material is prohibited. No part of this book may be reproduced or transmitted in any form or by any means, electronic or mechanical, including photocopying, recording, or by any information storage and retrieval system without express written permission from the author / publisher.

David Traub
David@SellBrilliantly.com

To my wonderful wife. Dawn, the best friend, wife and partner I could have ever hoped for.

To Alexander, my blind archer, you've been fighting since even before you were born. Your dedication and determination to accomplish your goals inspires me every day.

Introduction	1
The Five Secrets of Top-Performing Sellers	6
Secret #1: Following a System	6
Secret #2: Spending Time Brilliantly	10
Secret #3: Get Rid of the Junk Quickly	15
Secret #4: Closing More Business Faster	19
Secret #5: Learning Continuously	20
The Four-and-a-Half-Step Sales System	22
Prepare	25
Position and Attract	36
Ask Powerful Questions	46
Pitch, Overcome Objections, and Close	59
Follow Up	74
Common Questions and Pitfalls	85
How do I get more appointments?	86
Should I leave a voicemail?	90
How can I more effectively use email?	94
How do I create urgency in my prospect?	100
How can I find more time to sell	104
Recommended Reading	112

Introduction

As a business owner, coach, consultant or independent professional, you are your own sales team; and becoming a great seller is critical to your success. However, sales skills may be something you don't feel you have, or you may even feel that you can't sell altogether.

I'm going to show you proven, practical and easy-to-implement strategies to get more and better prospects, spend less time with tire-kickers and lead more people to take action on your offer faster than ever before, all without being pushy or salesy. As a result of using these strategies, you will double or even triple your sales over the next six to eleven months; some people can even do it in as little as 30 days.

The reality is that most professional salespeople are not any better at it than you are. The 20% of professional salespeople that get 80% of the results are all taking advantage of a sales success formula that garners them great results. When you learn to follow this formula – and I'll show you the best way to do that – you'll find that, even with your limited time as a business owner, you are able to sell effectively. In fact, you will even be capable of getting better results than most full-time salespeople.

This same formula applies to all areas of life; I first became aware of it from a great team of doctors. They didn't apply it to selling – they were using it in their practice of medicine – but the same formula applies almost everywhere.

At our first prenatal visit, my wife and I heard from our doctors that it may be too early to hear the baby's heartbeat, but that they were going to try anyway. After giving it a listen, the doctor said that no, she didn't hear anything, but as long as we were here, she'd call down and see if they might be able to sneak us in for a quick ultrasound. What we didn't know at the time was that at a busy hospital, you didn't just sneak in at the last minute for an ultrasound... they were looking for something in particular.

After the ultrasound, we went back up to see the doctor and she said that though everything looked okay, there was a little bit of an abnormality. She didn't want us to worry about it, but asked that we take a visit to see a specialist. So the next day, we whisked ourselves up to see one of the top high-risk specialist groups in the Chicago land area... and it was there that we learned that we were actually pregnant with twins.

Due to some odd fluke of nature, though, the twins were sharing an umbilical cord; and with this particular idiosyncrasy, there was typically an 80% chance that one baby will ultimately end up killing the other baby. What had happened was that one of our children was acting as the cardiovascular system for both, and, as a result, that baby likely would not be able to withstand the pressure of providing blood flow to both systems.

The procedure that had typically been used in these situations in and of itself had huge risks associated with it and in more than 50% of the cases, it resulted in the death of both babies. The baby that was not operating as the cardiovascular system (actually because of a lack of nutrients that were making it all the way to its system) had no chance of survival and would definitely die, but might ultimately kill the other, known as the *pump twin*.

Needless to say, we were beyond distraught. Our doctors, though, did not give up, and four weeks later, we ended up flying to Pittsburgh. Eventually my wife underwent an experimental procedure that resulted in my amazing son Alexander being born six months later.

The reason I tell you this story here is that the doctors followed a formula that saved my son's life... and it's that same exact formula that is just as critical to the life of your business. It amounts to the fact that the doctors were all very smart, they applied lots of effort to the problem and they were great at what they did. My son being born was a result of all three; not any one factor. So that overall formula for success is

Sales Success = Smarts x Effort x Quality

or as I sometimes refer to it, **SmEQ**. To get great sales results in your business, you must sell smarter; sell better; sell more.

In the last 23 years as a top-producing salesperson, I've learned what every top performer does differently than the rest... and I will share those things with you. Each and every one of them relates directly to selling smarter, selling better and selling more. Every top performer knows that to get great results, you've got to follow a sales system. If you're not following a sales system, you're not going to get top results, you can't analyze what parts of what you're doing need to be improved and it becomes almost impossible to replicate the successes that you do have.

As a result, you don't know what's working, what isn't and what needs to be fixed or what you need to do more of and what you need to do less of. By implementing systemization of your sales and your business, you will dramatically increase the effectiveness of the time you focus on driving revenue.

Next: all top performers sell more; and by "sell more" here, I don't mean that they're selling more of their products or services than other people. That will naturally come when you apply all the pieces of the success formula. What I mean is that they drive the sales more. Top performers are focusing their efforts on activities that generate sales, while average or low performers may spend lots of time working. Not all of that work – in fact, often very little of it – is actually focused on the few key activities that are going to drive their sales success.

I know that as a business owner, you are putting a lot of time, effort and energy into your business; you're probably working really long hours. What I find often, though, when I'm working with clients is that while they're working hard and they're working long hours, very little of that time is dedicated to selling; it's focused on delivering great services to their customers but very little on the actual selling.

How much of each day are you spending talking to prospective clients? Often, the quickest and easiest way to sell more of your products and services is literally to sell more. If you don't have as much money coming into your business as you would like, start re-doing your day and spending every minute possible on sales and business development activities. Take a hard look at what you do each day and find out what is critical to your business success and what's just nice; and start replacing those nice things with sales activities.

To start, I'd recommend that you target spending 80% of your time on these activities until you absolutely can't maintain that level. Only then do you begin to pull back. Later, I'll show you some great ways to make sure you're focusing your time on the right activities with the right prospects.

Part of the power of selling more is also that automatically, the more you sell, the better you are going to get at it; generally, the more time you spend at something, the better you get. And selling better is the final part of the formula. By putting more focus on selling, you're going to learn to improve your sales skills.

The top sellers in the world are skilled at speeding up the sales cycle at every opportunity, and one great way of doing that is to get rid of unlikely prospects faster. Some prospects drag out the decision-making process. You finish one sales conversation and they want you to call back next week, next month or next quarter. Average sellers play along and call back in a week or a month or a quarter, only to find that then, the phone tag starts or the chasing begins. It wastes your valuable time and often, it's wasting your time on prospects who ultimately will never buy.

Top sellers don't do this. They sift out these unlikely prospects fast. Determine quickly if the prospect is worth the time of another call, and if they are, we'll schedule the necessary follow-ups for a specific date and time. We'll touch much more on this later; but for now, just realize that scheduling the next call will tell you tons about the likelihood of that next contact happening with your prospect.

In *Team of One*, I'll outline for you some of my best strategies for making sure that you are selling smarter; selling better; selling more.

The Five Secrets of Top-Performing Sellers

One of the most common questions that I get asked is simply this: "How do I get more business?" It's really a loaded question because there's a lot that goes into it. But in essence, I have found that the top sellers, the best sellers in the world, all do some of the same things. Essentially, there really are five secrets that the top sellers in the world all do differently and better than everyone else.

Secret #1: Following a System

The first and perhaps the most important secret is that they follow a system: they don't go haphazardly about their sales day; about their sales process; about their selling. They follow a very specific system. Early in my sales career, after leaving a successful stint at IBM, I went to work for a company that did computer training all around the world. We taught everything from how to use a computer and the very basics (for example, the difference between clicking and double-clicking), all the way up to developing high-end server-based applications.

A couple of weeks in to this job, I got a call from my manager. He'd asked if he could see me for a minute and I told him

I'd be right in. I went down to his office and he started up the conversation by saying, "It looks like this may not be working out," – that certainly was not what I expected to hear from my new boss. It was barely the third week after finishing the training program and I was still very excited by the job, the training program. On my first day on the phones, I had tried (and succeeded) to close a deal that was worth 25% of my quota for the first month.

I had been successful in my sales jobs in the past and I was getting along with everyone here. I was off to a good start; or at least, so I thought. They seemed to have had a different impression.

The problem was that yes, I closed a full 25% of my quota on the first day, but it now was a little over two and a half weeks later… and I hadn't sold anything else. It was pretty expected in this job that you'd have sales coming in on a regular basis, even out of the gate. There was a ramp up where it would need to grow. But even in that first month, they expected that you'd be closing business right away, and I hadn't closed anything since that first day. Now, two and a half weeks later, my daily forecast still showed up with a big fat zero.

To top it off, I hadn't hit three other key metrics from the previous week. There were other things that they measured and I was falling behind on those as well. He took the time to take me back through the job requirements, reminded me of my quota, and pointed out that I still had eight full days left before the end of the month. So I still had plenty of time to turn things around.

Then he asked me if there was anything else that he could do to help. I was in a bit of shock and at the time, said no. In my head, I was thinking that what he could do was just back off, let me do my job; I have proven myself in the past; I know that I can do this. But I didn't say that out loud. I knew that he had hired me because I had a history of being able to sell, and that making me stress out over it wasn't going to work. None of that, of course, was going to be very helpful.

What was helpful, though, was that he did connect me with one of the top reps in the company out of another office, and we talked for a bit about what was going on, how I was doing, how I was going about my day, etc. She had really focused me in on a very specific system that has not only been successful for her, but also for this company and for many people around the world. Yes, they had taught it to me in training... but I thought that I knew better. She showed me otherwise; she got me back into following the system.

The bottom line is, over the next eight days, I focused myself on working very hard and very carefully following the system; doing exactly what had been laid out; which, again and again and again, has been successful for others across the company.

As a result of doing that, I not only came in 25% above quota for that first month, I actually I elected to make the jump from a base salary into a full commission position, four months early! This is something that during the ramp, everybody would have to do eventually; but normally, it took around nine months to get there. I elected to make that change several months early because that compensation plan was more lucrative at my production level even without a base salary.

Not only that, but in my ninth month in the company, I had actually hit a sales volume that got me a promotion into a senior account executive, and it was the first time in the Chicago office that anyone had ever done it in less than a calendar year. Several more years than I care to admit later, that record still has not been broken, and I went on to become one of the top 5% of reps in a company with over 2,000 reps worldwide. It all was because I followed these five secrets and, very particularly, this specific sales system; and it doesn't just work in that industry and with that training. Following the system works everywhere.

One of the most recognized companies in the world, which only started in 1940, began in a single location. In 1955, the owners of that business sold out to a businessman, and the new owner immediately started documenting and systemizing everything in the business. And 59 years later, that one location now has turned into having over 34,000 locations around the world in over 118 countries. They employ over 1.7 million people around the world and every year for the last 25 years, they have exceeded their shareholder dividends. They have revenues over $27.5 billion a year and profits exceeding $5.5 billion a year.

If you haven't figured it out already, the company that I'm talking about is McDonald's. Roy Crock's systemization of everything in their business, right down to how their cashiers sell French fries, has made them one of the most recognized names in the world. Every time you go into a McDonald's store, even if you order just a sandwich, they ask if you would like fries with that. As a result, they sell millions of dollars of French fries every year. If you don't order dessert, they'll ask, "Would you like an apple pie with that?" They sell millions of pies every year.

A very small piece of the puzzle for them is that overall, as an organization, systemizing even the sales of your business can have dramatic results for you. Later, I will share with you my simple four-and-a-half-step sales process that has led to my closing tens of millions of dollars in sales personally and helped those that I've coached and trained close over $100 million of business.

Secret #2: Spending Time Brilliantly

Secret number two is that top sellers spend their time brilliantly. They have found great ways of making sure that they're super productive with their time; they're making time and focusing that time on the high revenue-producing activities and doing things that are specifically designed to have an impact on their business. They make time to sell every day; they make time to find new prospects and new clients to talk to every day; and they make sure that every day, they have systems in place which keep them on track for doing exactly that.

That means spending every possible minute on generating leads, working those leads through to setting appointments and eventually closing the sale... and then following up to get referrals and additional business from them. You should really be focusing as much of your time as possible on sales and marketing. Many people who are business owners or coaches or consultants spend the bulk of their day – every day – on delivering great results for their clients, and very little time, if any, on selling.

What I'd recommend that you do is to make sure that you are spending time every day on generating new business. Ideally, you should set aside time every day for sales and marketing activities, and then you should break up that time into individual segments. Spend 40% of that time on closing business, protecting your base of clients and growing your base of clients. That could involve taking meetings with and talking to eminent buyers (including those people who are likely to buy soon and potential clients who've expressed an interest and taken action towards doing business with you), and meeting with and talking to current customers of yours about referrals or about growing the existing business that you're doing with them. But that doesn't mean just talking to them about how your current project is going; it also involves specifically talking about new or expanded business.

Then you should be spending 40% or more of your sales time towards looking for new business. You should always be prospecting. Prospecting does not necessarily mean cold-calling, but it does mean doing the things that lead to setting new appointments and talking to new customers or new potential customers, folks who've not done business with you before. You should be spending at least 40% of your sales time doing that.

When you get to a point where you're really busy and you have a lot of customers, it's easy forget about prospecting because you think you are doing well. You may be doing well then, but it's because of the energy you put before into getting new customers. When you stop, it will ultimately have a significant downward effect on your business.

I experienced this personally (and very dramatically) a number of years ago. It was at that same company where I was nearly fired in my first month. But several months later, I worked really hard; I had a particular goal that I was trying to hit and, eventually, things worked out really well. What ended up happening at one point is that I grew the business to a point where, for the first time in my life, I took home what I considered to be a very substantial pay-check. I had had some five-figure pay-checks before; but now I had jumped up a level and got a pay-check for $29,000 for one month's work. I was absolutely thrilled; things were going fantastic; business couldn't have been better.

30 days later, I got my next pay-check for $2,000. So I had had a $27,000 drop in my income in 30 days, and that was because for the ninety days or so prior to that, I had been focusing all of my time and energy on closing business and working with my existing clients and projects that were already in the works. I hadn't been spending time – or anywhere near enough time – prospecting for

new business because I didn't feel that I needed it; things were going really well. Well, when all of that business that was in my pipeline dried up and was closed or lost, my income dropped tremendously.

So I highly advise you that, no matter how good things are going, you should carve off time and make sure that you are prospecting for new business. There are lots of ways that you can do that. Cold-calling is one. A lot of people don't like it (including a lot of seasoned salespeople) but it still can be very successful. It's not my preferred way, though. There are lots of ways that you can do warm-calling. The bottom line, though, is: "Always be prospecting."

The only time that you should stop prospecting and finding ways of getting new business is when you have so much new business coming to you automatically because of your positioning and marketing that you have enough people coming to you on their own, ready to do business with you, that you're having to turn away business and you can't take on new projects because you're too busy. Until you reach that point, you need to continue to prospect. Remember, rules number one, two and three when it comes to prospecting is: "Always be prospecting".

You can be focused on getting speaking engagements. When you've positioned yourself as an expert, you can do speaking engagements in front of small and large crowds. It changes your entire positioning, and it leads people to want to talk to you more about what it is that you're doing or how it can impact your business. You naturally end up in a position with lots of relationships with people who become prospects for you.

The bottom line, though, is that you should spend every extra minute on prospecting for new business that you can find; anything you can carve out of your day that's not generating revenue for you. Refocusing on prospecting for new business will reward you tremendously in the long run.

Ask yourself, "Do I have an effective sales plan for my day?" or "Do I have one at all?"

Unfortunately, I see a lot of business owners and salespeople just bounce through their day, doing whatever it is that comes up next. They're completely at the mercy of their prospects that happen to say something or do something that day; they're completely at the mercy of whatever bounces into their mind at that particular time, without having planned out ahead of time what's the highest priority for them, what's the highest paying activity for them to do in any given day and throughout particular times of that day.

Oftentimes, I see coaches and consultants go from appointment to appointment without any plan of how they're going to use the downtime in between appointments. Ultimately, that ends up in a whole lot of procrastination, oftentimes on Facebook or social media or reading news or calling low-value prospects instead of high-value ones. So you need to spend as much time as possible on focusing specifically on what's going to bring in new business or on closing deals that are already in your pipeline.

I've said it before, but it can never be said enough that you should always be prospecting. Every week, every day, you need to have time that you put on your calendar that is set aside for prospecting, and you need to continue to do this up until you get to a point where you have so many paying projects lined up that you have to start turning away business. Even then, you should still continue to have some prospecting on your calendar. You may just not do it every day, but try to maintain some level of prospecting, even at your busiest moments, because eventually, the stuff that's in your pile will dry up.

Your prospecting time should be as important as any client appointment, so schedule a time at the beginning of a month or the beginning of the week or even the beginning of the day. Pull out your calendar and put on it exactly when you are going to be doing prospecting activities. This should be happening at least three times a week, although I'd recommend ideally that you carve out some time prospecting every day.

Prospecting time does not mean necessarily that you're cold-calling. Prospecting time can be spent calling warm leads; it can be spent calling people who can book you for speaking engagements; it can be spent calling past customers to ask for referrals. But specifically, it is simply time that you're spending in your business on activities that will directly lead to getting new business and new leads coming into your company.

Anything that can lead to engaging a new business is considered prospecting. However, activities that aren't ultimately going to lead to new business do not constitute prospecting and you need to make sure that these do not fall within your prospecting time. Also, to make sure that you're getting the most out of your prospecting time and that the leads and the calls that you make seem to be moving forwards, ensure that every time you're ending a call or a meeting that there's another call that's going to be required. Schedule it then. Don't just leave it as, "Let's talk next week." It's too much time wasted playing phone tag. You have to value your time enough to schedule each and every call.

Secret #3: Get Rid of the Junk Quickly

The third secret is that they get rid of the junk faster. Many people spend a lot of time selling (or so they think), but really they're just spending a lot of their time talking to customers who will never buy from them. They either aren't qualified to make the decision, don't have the dollars to make the decision or ultimately just are not really all that interested in doing business or solving the problems that you've talked to them about. They may be willing to talk to you, but they aren't going to turn ultimately into business. The top performers find ways (and there are systems for doing that) of identifying the people who are not likely to do business with them and subsequently, they spend less and less time with them.

At one point in my career, I was managing a sales team – it was the same company that I talked about previously. I had left the company and come back as a sales manager. So one of my previous peers ended up being one of my employees; he was a great sales rep and he'd been historically doing really well with the company. He, however, had been in a several-month slump. We spent some time sitting down, going through all of the accounts that he was working on and all of the opportunities that he was working on. What became clear is that he had too many people that he was talking to on a regular basis about business which consistently just did not turn into customers.

We took him from handling and working with 300 different accounts on prospective deals and handed off 210 of those to other people in the organization to follow up on. This left him with 90 accounts; 90 potential customers that he was going to work with. It took less than 30 days for his sales volume to go from $80,000 to $140,000 a month. He nearly doubled his business in 30 days simply by getting rid of more than half of the people that he was trying to sell to. Finding ways of getting rid of the people who ultimately are wasting your time, as counterintuitive as it seems, will grow your business.

It's pretty common for people to constantly call the same prospects over and over again. However, there are prospects and leads that may be wasting your time. While you should never give up on a lead until they tell you to go away – and some people would say not even then – you do need to prioritize whom you're spending your active time on, so what you should look for is who is wasting your time.

Early in my sales career, I had a phrase that was drilled into my head: "Close or dump." In this case, when it was taught to me, it was very hardcore. When they talked about "close or dump" at this company, they literally talked about dumping them out of your database; you would delete all of your notes, the people's names, their phone numbers, their email address.

This was way before email marketing was popular and they just clearly didn't understand the value of the database. But the point was: Don't spend your time on people who are not going to be moving forwards with you.

So what I have taken this to mean over the course of my career is that I'm looking at closing; not necessarily always the sale itself, but closing in on the next step or constantly moving forwards in the sale. It doesn't just involve the person saying, "Okay, we can talk again next week"; they need to be taking some sort of action along the way, demonstrating that they actually truly are interested. They need to show that they're not just willing to talk to you again or at least say that they're willing to talk to you again, solely in order to get you off the phone.

They need to take some sort of action; this could be

reviewing the report that you send them, or coordinating a meeting with somebody else in their office, or giving you some financial numbers that you need in order to be able to have the next discussion with them and to plan for that meeting accordingly... but they need to be taking action.

Customers who are not taking action and not doing anything are the first ones that you should be looking to move out of your active files. But as long as a prospect continues to take action, and they're moving forwards, I typically continue to work with them and continue to try to actively sell towards them.

We talked before about spending your time brilliantly; one important point here is that you need to be focusing not just on the activities that are likely to generate revenue; you need to be looking even deeper than that. Prioritize your time and focus on the prospects or the leads that are most likely going to make you money. Take a long, hard look at whom you're calling, and start cutting back when people aren't taking action.

Don't give up too soon though. In general, on any new lead, you should make at least six to nine calls before giving up reaching the contact. A common contact ratio these days is 10%. What that means is that every ten times you make a phone call, you will connect with who you are calling only one time. That goes for all calls, not just initial prospecting calls.

You should never, however, stop contacting your prospects until they do tell you to go away; but what you can do, is to let technology take over. So once you've determined that a prospect is not someone that you're actively going to be calling on a regular basis in order to try to get additional business out of them, you still should continue to use a system that will send emails or deliver text messages and even send voicemails automatically for you, to those prospects.

I highly encourage you to look at the automated service, Instant Customer, at <u>www.instantcustomer.com</u>. It's a great system that will allow you to capture leads in a number of different places as well as send emails, voicemails and text messages to your prospects automatically. You can set them up in a sequence, or you can send out broadcasts to everyone in a group that meets certain conditions at a particular time. It's a great way to continue to contact these clients en masse without you having to pay individual attention to them.

Secret #4: Closing More Business Faster

Secret number four is that they close more business faster. Now you may be thinking, "Oh, boy, that sounds obvious. The people who are closing the most business are doing it faster than others." Well, yes, but it's not just a natural thing that is happening; it is because they are specifically finding ways and focusing on the things that cause more business to happen faster. They tend to have a higher average deal size; they're always looking for ways to increase the amount of business that each project is doing. They're not just closing small deals; they are making it obvious for their customers that it's in their benefit to do larger deals.

They also look for ways to drive sales forwards on every contact with that customer. It's not uncommon for me to hear people closing calls or meetings with their customers with a very awkward, undefined next step: "We'll talk in a couple weeks," "We'll talk in a month," or whatever it is. But what's not happening is having a specific time and date for a next conversation to happen.

You're not necessarily asking for the deal to close, but if there's a reason for you to continue contact with that customer, just simply taking the act of scheduling that call will make the whole process move along faster. Also, when you are scheduling that next call, I recommend that you ask for mini-commitments. Maybe they're not going to sign the contract right away, but you can ask them to do something – review some materials, do some internal research, get you new numbers – something that demonstrates they're willing to take action. And doing that on every call will have a tremendous impact on how quickly those deals happen for you.

Secret #5: Continually be learning

The final secret is that they're always learning. The top performers in sales are always focused on improving their sales goals. They go to seminars; they read books; they practice their pitches. That's something that you just don't see the average performers doing. It's something that you should be doing in your business.

You may be spending a lot of time on learning how to run your medical practice, you may be spending time learning how to be a better chiropractor, you may be doing all kinds of continuing education on whatever it is your core business is; but you must start learning to improve your sales skills and continue to do so. There's very little that you can do in your business that will have higher impact on your revenue than learning to get more and better leads and close those sales faster.

In fact, at one company that I worked for, we went to a national conference which attracted some of the top sales performers from around the country once a year. At that conference, one year, I and a couple other people went around and took some surveys of the people that were in the top half of the top performers in that organization. There were a number of things that we asked, but one of those things was: "What is it that you have been doing in the last 14 days prior to the conference to improve your sales skills?"

We found that even among these top performers, the top 20% had dramatically different results than the rest. All of those also had focused on improving their sales skills in the last 14 days. What we actually found was that every one of the people who had done something to improve their skills within the last 14 days was outperforming everybody else that we had surveyed by more than double. This seems to be the case in almost every organization.

When you take a look at the people who are getting the best sales results, it doesn't matter that they're already getting the best sales results; they still are doing things to improve their sales skills on a regular basis. You're taking a great first step by reading *Team of One* to start yourself on the path of learning great sales skills.

Later in the book, in one of the appendixes, I will list some of my recommendations for the best sales training material out there, so that you can implement it into your own sales team of one.

To recap, here are the five secrets of top-performing sellers:

1. Following a Systems

2. Spending Time Brilliantly

3. Tossing out the Junk Quickly

4. Closing more Business Faster

5. Learning Continuously

Bonus: Follow-up automation in action

Want to try out my favorite follow up automating tool. Text **#FOLLOWUP** to (847) 380-8117 and I'll send you a special link where you can get a $1 trial of my favorite follow up automation tool. It's simply and powerful. Plus you can automat your social media posts, and distribute content to multiple video sites.

The Four-and-a-Half-Step Sales System

The Four-and-a-Half-Step Sales System

Michael Gerber, who wrote the bestselling business book *The E-Myth Revisited: Why Most Small Businesses Don't Work and What to Do About It*, talks a lot in that book about systems. His ideas have helped thousands of businesses all over the world, and systemization is one of the most important factors that he discusses.

> "Things need to be sold. And it's usually people who have to sell them. Everyone in business has heard the old saw: 80% of our sales are produced by 20% of our people. Unfortunately, few seem to know what the 20% are doing that the 80% are not. Well, let me tell you. The 20% are using a system and the 80% are not. A selling system is a soft system. And I've seen such systems produce 100% to 500% increases in sales in almost no time! What is a selling system? It's a fully orchestrated interaction between you and your customer" – **Michael Gerber**

Systemizing your business is not just about making sure that you have the proper processes and procedures in place to deliver your product or services in an easy manner to your customers; you must also systemize your sales process. It's actually critical to the success of your business, especially because, considering the limited amount of selling time that you have as a business owner, one of the ways that you can get the biggest and quickest increases in your business is to go through systematizing your sales process.

Now, I have a very easy-to-use sales system that I, personally, and hundreds of those that I've coached, have used to generate tens of millions of dollars of sales. It consists of four-and-a-half steps.

Step one is to **prepare**. Set yourself up for success properly. Just like an iceberg has much of its mass below the surface – it's something that you never see – the same is true of your sales. Your customers, your prospects, will likely never see much of what you need to do to ensure your success in the start of the sales process.

You also need to **position and attract** yourself. This is where you'll position yourself as an expert and as someone that they want to do business with. You'll position your business, attract clients to you and set appointments with them to go into in-depth discussions of how you can help them or their businesses.

Then in that appointment, in that meeting or that phone call, you'll move onto **asking powerful questions**. This is so critical to the success of your business and of your sales that it is its own step within the process. Believe it or not, more sales are won or lost in this step of the sales cycle than any other part of the system. There are a lot of things that you can do, or cannot do, that may cause you to lose a sale, but questioning is undoubtedly one of the biggest impacts that you can have on your sales processes;

simply by learning to ask the right questions and the powerful questions.

Then the next step is to **pitch, handle objections, and close the sale**. That's all one step of the cycle: pitching, handling the objection and closing the sale, because they're all so integrated. It's one of the areas that many people are fearful of and think that they're not good at. But when you're following a system, and you're asking powerful questions that lead to insightful conversations with your customers, you'll find that those conversations will naturally lead into pitching your solution, answering their questions, and ultimately asking for the business.

Then the fourth-and-a-half step is to **follow up**... and this doesn't come last; it's actually integrated throughout the whole process. Following up is not really a step of its own, but it's something that you need to do every step of the way throughout the sales process, even well after the sale. It's so important that I wanted to list it out as a separate part of the process.

Overall, the system has 4.5 steps.

1. Prepare
2. Position and Attract
3. Ask Powerful Questions
4. Pitch, Overcome Objections, and Close
4.5. Follow Up

Prepare

The first thing in the sales process that I mentioned is prepare; and there's a lot that goes into the prepare category. It starts with the mindset at the beginning of all of it, and it also takes into account your goals, your scripting, your pricing, your research and your education and skills.

Mindset

The start of it all comes from mindset, and it's particularly important to talk about your mindset of sales. Many people, perhaps even you, feel negatively about sales and selling. You rarely find someone that thinks that when you ask them what they wanted to be when they were a kid, and they said, "Oh, I wanted to be a salesman." It's because many of you have a viewpoint of sales as being arm-twisting, high-pressure and manipulative; it reminds you of a used car salesmen and of being pushy.

If you have a negative viewpoint of selling, it will impact your own ability to get business. The truth is that top salespeople do not take that approach; they don't twist arms, they're not high-pressure, they're not manipulative and they definitely don't fit your stereotype of a used car salesman. They treat their sales and their selling as a conversation and as a service to their customers. They realize that selling is a conversation where you lead people through making a decision and taking action.

Take a second to stop and ask yourself these questions:

- Do I offer a quality product or service?
- Does what I offer provide great benefit to my customers?
- Are my customers better off with what I provide to them than without it?

- Will the benefits I bring to my customers through my products or services improve the quality of their businesses or their lives?
- Do I operate with honesty and integrity with my customers?

Now, if you answered "yes" to those questions, I want you to stop and realize that by not maximizing your sales skills and your sales efforts, you are actually cheating those customers out of the benefits that you have to offer. It is actually a disservice to your customers or your potential customers to not maximize your sales skills and not put everything that you can into your sales process and get customers to do business with you. Only when you realize that, can you begin to change. That change needs to start with the language that you use with yourself.

Many people who don't focus on the sales in their business may say things to themselves like, "I'm not good enough," "I'm not good at sales," "I'm not a salesman," "I'm not worth it," "I hate talking on the phone," "I'm not good at recruiting," or "I'm not good at asking for the business." If you find yourself saying any of those things to yourself, you need to stop it now. Just stop it.

One great way of doing that is to start reprogramming your mind by having powerful affirmations that are in support of what it is that you want. What I'd like to see you do is find anywhere from three to eight, or write your own affirmations and put them on a piece of paper or on a card or on your iPad, your phone, whatever it is that you have, that you can keep with you. And every day, early in the morning, before bed, and if possible, a couple of times throughout the day, repeat those affirmations to yourself. You will find over time that you start to incorporate those into your life, and it will dramatically change the way you think of yourself and your sales abilities.

Here are some examples:
- Today I will create immense value for the people around me and earn a profit proportionate to that action.
- Today I will work XXX and make $$$.
- Today I will focus ENTIRELY on what I give, instead of what I get.
- I will give everything my undivided attention and commitment, and work to my maximum ability.
- Here are 300 affirmations that you can use in many ways
- I am successful in everything I do.
- I have clearly defined goals and I will pursue them today with enthusiasm, determination and discipline.
- I will see failure as only a signpost on my road to success.
- I see every problem as an opportunity to overcome a challenge.
- I never take rejection personally. I am first and foremost in the people business. I realize that they can only reject my proposal, not me. I keep on keepin' on.
- Today, when I feel stress, I will consciously relax and let go of my stress before making the next call.
- The excellence of my service will determine the level of my income.
- Today, I'll give more than ever before.
- I am determined to work harder on myself than on my job. This way I can become the person I want to be and end up doing a better job than ever before.
- Selling is the country's most important profession for creating new wealth. It is the foundation of the free enterprise system.
- I am a professional problem solver and I care more about my prospects than making the sale.
- It does not matter what I want to sell, what matters

is what my prospect wants to own.
- I call my best prospects first
- I am disciplined and focused on today's greatest opportunities.
- In sales, business and in my personal life I am only handed challenges that I am capable of achieving.
- Each and every call I make I start with an incredible level of positive expectation and prosperity I know that right now somewhere someone's life is better and more prosperous because of my products and services.
- I am joyfully receiving wealth and abundance in my life.
- I am creating money in my life.
- It is great to have money.
- I am ready for abundance.
- Money enhances my positive power.
- I love life.
- I am a loving person.
- My life is a success story.
- I am successful in everything I do.
- I am willing and daring to go all the way.
- I will reach my goals, joyfully and easily.
- I am always reaching my goals in one way or another.
- I am joyfully receiving wealth and abundance in my life.
- I am moving towards money.
- I am creating money in my life.
- It is great to have money.
- I am creating riches to share with the whole world because it is my joy to share.
- Every day and in every way I am getting better and better.
- I am choosing to make the time to take control of my sales.

Goals

Another part of preparation is having goals. You need to make sure that you have goals, not just about what you want out of your life, but very specifically, about your goals for your sales within your business. They help you drive and focus your mind. You should have a series of goals about how much business that you want to get; how many customers that you want to have; how many people's lives you want to impact with your products or services.

Before you respond and say, "Yes, I have those things", stop and ask yourself, "Are they written down, and are they specific? Are they powerful? Are they something that make me want to stretch myself?" If they are not, go back and write them down – and make sure that they are powerful.

Once you have a list of goals written down, you need to go back and also write down, for each goal: why that goal is important to you, why you want it, what it will do for you and how it will impact your life. Then once you've done that, go back through, and for each one, write down: what will happen if you don't get the goal, what it will mean for you if you don't accomplish that goal, what will happen, how it will impact your life, how it will impact your family and what you will feel if you don't attain that goal.

I promise you that by doing this for each of the goals – not just around your sales, but each of the goals for your life – the process will dramatically improve the likelihood that you will follow through and do what's necessary in order to attain those goals.

Pricing

Pricing is another thing you should prepare. I understand that different deals may have different pricing structures, but you should know up-front what pricing models you plan on using, and you should know how you value your own time. You should know up-front that part of your pricing is made up of your own time; you need to take into consideration how much time you'll spend on each deal and how much your time is worth.

If you haven't gone through an exercise in understanding what your rate needs to be in order to hit the sales goals, the income goals that you have, you may find that you're pricing yourself out of reach of those goals. To figure out the minimum amount you need to quote for your time take your income goal and divide it by 2,000 (40 hours x 50 weeks). If you quote your time for any less than that you will not make your income goal. For example if you want to make at least $250,000 / year you'll need to charge at least $125 for every hour of your time.

Research

Part of preparation also comes from research. You need to make sure that you have researched your market, what your competitors are doing and what your customers actually want from you, from your products and from your services. Don't just assume that you know what is going on in your marketplace or that you know what your competitors are doing, or, worst of all, what it is that your customers want.

You may be surprised to find that your customers are buying your products and services for reasons other than what you think. It's important that you spend some time researching what caused them to do business with you. It should be really simple to go back and ask a selection of your customers, "Why are you doing business with me? What is it that made you choose me?" Those insights will help you tremendously as you work on your scripts and as you ask questions and have conversations with customers.

Sales Script

One other common question that I get is, "Should I use a sales script?" And the answer is: absolutely, you should. I hear from a lot of people that they're not comfortable using a script and that they don't want to use a script mainly because it can take away from genuine conversation or it's going to make them sound salesy or pushy. That simply is untrue, not when it's done right.

If you simply read from a script word for word, don't take into account what people say and don't listen to what they're saying, then yes, that would be true. But that is not what top people do, and that's not what you're going to do. There's actually a formula to a script, and it allows for dialog; it allows for you to respond to what people say.

You should even plan out and script out what questions you'll ask. Have you ever finished a call with a potential client and realized that you forgot to ask something important? Well, it's because you didn't have your questions scripted. If you have written out what questions you want to ask, you will be much less likely to forget asking something important. You should plan out how you will explain certain things.

You've probably had the experience where you've tried explaining the same thing multiple times to multiple people, and each time you explain it, it's different. Sometimes people end up responding the way you want, sometimes they don't. When you're not using a script, you won't be able to tell what wording is working and what isn't, because you're being haphazard in the way that you're explaining everything.

A script is really just a plan for your conversation. You want to use the best words that you can so that you learn what works and what doesn't, and then keep updating those scripts accordingly. Break everything down into small little scripts, not a big one. It makes it easier to plan and to cut and paste and move things around on the fly when it becomes necessary. There are a whole lot of different types of scripts that you're going to have, too.

For instance, you'll have a script for the opening of your prospecting calls. You should script out how you will ask for the order, what questions you'll ask in what order, and how you'll respond to particular questions and objections. By knowing what to say before you get in front of someone, before you get in front of a group, or before you pick up your phone, you will quickly catapult your sales numbers.

For example, have you ever had a conversation where you know what you're trying to say, but it's clear you can't get the point out, and the person you're talking to doesn't understand? I know I've had that experience, and it's really because the order that I'm putting my ideas in and the words I'm using just don't make sense to my listener. Occasionally, it may not even make sense to me. You may not realize it, but your prospect feels all of that; the words you use, and the order in which you use them, make a difference.

A script, according to Webster, is simply a plan of action. Really, it's a simple sequence of words that makes sense. Think about it this way: If you try to make cheesy scrambled eggs, you follow the same routine every time; you're going to use the same ingredients each time you make it; you're going to go in the same order every time. You're not going to turn on the stove, put the pan on the stove, put the cheese in the pan, go to the fridge to get the eggs, sprinkle the cheese with pepper, then crack the eggs into a bowl and put the shells in the pan. It just doesn't make sense.

If you don't use a script, that is exactly what you are doing when you try to sell someone your products or your services. It may not be complete gibberish, but the words or the ingredients that you are using might not be quite right, or they're used in the wrong order to achieve maximum impact. When you make cheesy eggs, you follow a recipe. The same thing is true when you're trying to sell your products or services. You should use a recipe; use a script.

Sometimes, it's the very little things that matter, and I've seen more than one chef sent home from *Top Chef* or other cooking competitions for under-salting something. Just don't take the chance of doing the same thing with your sales prospects. Don't send your prospects homes without giving them the best that you have to offer.

When it comes to scripts, there are a number of basic scripts that you should create. You should have a script for your opening prospecting call. You should have a script for opening warm-calls, a voicemail script. Don't be caught off guard when you get someone's voicemail. Know what you're going to say ahead of time: script for how you're going to handle particular objections; what questions you're going to ask your prospect; your closing; have a script for setting appointments; a script for asking for referrals.

For example, this has worked very well for a number of sales reps I know when asking for referrals. They'll say, "As you probably know, I work with referrals. A great referral for me is..." and then explain what makes someone a great customer for you. In my case, it may be a business owner who does not have a sales team. When you think of a good referral, think of people like that;

business clients that you have, people you've met at other events or people from mastermind groups.

"Of everyone that you know, who do you think would be the best referral for me?" That script, or something very similar, works really well. It's not telling people that you like referrals and asking them whether they can think of someone who would be a good fit. You explain to them what makes someone a good fit. Give them ideas of what to think about, and then ask who the best one is. It puts a lot of focus in the direction that you're looking.

Scripting out their sales process is exactly what every top sales superstar does, and you should do the same exact thing in your business.

Education

Another part of preparation is your education, and we've already talked a bit about the fact that you should always be learning. One of the five secrets of the very best top performers is to always be learning. Tony Robbins talks about it consistently; he talks about constant and never-ending improvement.

You should ask yourself, "Has my income been growing every year?" If it has not, ask yourself: "Has my education around improving my marketing and sales been consistent every year?" You may find a correlation between the two answers; you may find that you haven't been educating yourself on an ongoing basis and focusing on the sales and marketing part of your business, and as a result, your income has not been growing.

There's literally no skill that's more important in your business than your ability to generate leads and convert those leads into sales. It should be something that you are doing every day. I can't stress it enough: **always be learning and always focus on improving your sales and marketing skills.** You need to realize that you need to improve both. Just getting consistently better at marketing your business is not necessarily going to translate into closing more deals; you need to focus on both parts of the puzzle here. You need to focus on getting more leads, and then on converting those leads into customers by improving your sales skills.

In the appendix, you'll find a list of some of the best sales and marketing books that you should be reading in order to improve those skills. Also, on my website, you will find that same list with links to pick up those books on Amazon. That list is updated on a regular basis as I find new books that will help you close more business.

Position and Attract

After preparation, the next step in the sales process is position and attract. Now in the older and more traditional sales model, typically what would come here is cold-calling, which is calling up businesses and people that you think could be in need of your service and pitching it to them completely cold, with them having no idea who you are or that you would be calling.

This cold-calling still can be very effective. However, it is quite time-consuming as you need to make lots and lots of phone calls or physical door knocks in order to find a qualified candidate for your products or services. There are much better ways in today's marketplace to start having conversations with qualified prospects.

The process of doing that starts with positioning. Ideally, you should be doing things that are positioning you as an expert in your niche or positioning your business as the best choice for your service. When you properly position and attract customers, you actually have the ability to build rapport with prospects even before you meet them. Prospects are much more likely to do business with people who they know, like and trust; and positioning yourself or your business as an expert helps speed that process along.

There are a number of ways that you can get prospects to come to you, essentially by raising their hands and saying that they are interested in your products or services, without having to resort to just traditional advertising. Writing articles or blog posts that relate to your product or services and niche – particularly those that are providing solid information for your customers without directly trying to sell – is a great way of helping position yourself as an expert. In fact, you should probably be writing articles for your own website and blog as well as for guest posts that you may be doing on other blogs within your topic.

Also, one way to really position yourself as being the expert in your particular niche is to write a book. This may sound like it's a major task and sound scary, but it's actually relatively simple to do. There's a number of reasons why you want to do that. First of all, when it comes to being credible in your niche, there's very little that you can do that positions yourself so quickly as by being able to say that you are an author or a bestselling author in your particular niche.

There's a number of ways to go about getting your book written. One is to conduct a number of interviews and have those transcribed and assembled into a book. Another is to write an answer to the most common questions that you run into on your topic as well as the questions that are maybe not asked, and should be asked, and then transcribing those and compiling that into a book. In today's era, it's very simple to self-publish and get your book onto Amazon.

One of my mentors, Mike Koenigs, has a great and very easy-to-implement system for doing exactly this. He has a step-by-step system that you can use to get your book written, published and launched in under 30 days. It becomes the most powerful business card that you've ever had, and it's a fantastic lead generational tool, probably one of the best that you've ever used. You can find details about Mike's process for this by going to Bonus.TeamOfOneBook.com/publish

Once you've written and published a book, it becomes something that you can leverage when you're meeting clients and prospects. You can use it as a door opener by sending a copy of the physical book in the mail to prospects along with a handwritten note. When you're meeting for the first time with prospects, you can give them a copy. It tremendously raises the credibility of what it is you have to say, just by them knowing that you've written a book on the topic.

Then another fantastic thing to do is to speak on stage. It doesn't have to be a very big stage, but there's an instant credibility factor that comes from putting yourself out there and presenting on your topic. There may be some fear that you have with public speaking; but once you've gone out there and done this a couple of times, you begin to get your sea legs about it, and the fear goes away.

After you have presented on your topic to a group, you are immediately seen as the expert; and you'll find that after speaking (whether it be at business meet-ups or conventions or conferences in your market and in your niche), you will very frequently be approached by people who want to talk to you about what you had to say and how it applies to their business. This is a fantastic opportunity for you to generate leads by being a speaker.

All of these things – having the book, having the articles where you're really giving up yourself and giving content in teaching – these things lead to people connecting with you and them feeling like they know and like and trust you, even before you have an opportunity to speak to them individually. It becomes a great way of making sure that you are viewed differently than any of your competition.

Along with this, you need to make sure that you have a good way of capturing the leads that come from your book, from your articles and from your speaking engagements, and that you can consistently and automatically feed them more great content so that by capturing the lead, you'll know with whom to follow up. Also, by continuing to drip-feed additional content to them in an automated manner, those people you don't immediately connect with will continue to grow their sense of familiarity, affection and trust for you.

Now, there are a number of systems that you can use to do this. I recommend Instant Customer; I'll insert a link at the end of the chapter where you can actually get a free trial of Instant Customer. It is a fantastic system that will not only allow you to capture leads from your website, but also build specific lead generation pages for you that you can use to send people to your book, or to those articles of yours that are very targeted to the specific message that you are speaking or writing about.

It also allows people to opt in by texting their email to you. So when you are doing speaking engagements or you're meeting people at meet-ups or business conferences, you can simply have them text their email address to you to get this information from you. Instant Customer is a fantastic system; I highly recommend it.

Then the final part of positioning and attracting the customers is achieved by setting appointments with these people that you are meeting. There are a number of different things that you can do to get the ball rolling in the first appointment. The overall goal for you is to have a conversation; a deep-dive conversation with the prospect about their business or about themselves and what their needs are, and help them to understand how your products and services can satisfy those needs. Indeed, the first meeting or call really does revolve entirely around discovering their needs.

Some people may call these *initial consultations*; you may call it with your customer simply a *meeting*; you may call it a *free initial session*. There are a lot of things, depending on your market, by which you can call it. But the bottom line is that you're going to want to move into the question phase in that call and really get your customer talking about their needs, their desires and their wants, as well as the challenges that they may be running into. It's an initial sales call.

Through your lead process, you may implement a way of letting people self-schedule with you, so that you can set those appointments in an automated fashion. There are some tools that I'll recommend that you can use to do that, but you'll find a lot of times when you are speaking or when you've done your book and have provided people with a way of contacting you, that you will get people that reach out to you and say, "Hey, can we have a discussion about what it is that you said in Chapter 2? Can we have a discussion about how you might be able to help me with it in my business?"

You'll have some people that will self-schedule and say they specifically want to talk to you about it, and you'll want to go ahead and obviously schedule those conversations as quickly as possible. You can provide them a link to do scheduling online, or you can just send an email with your availability. You can do it however you like, but make sure you get those appointments scheduled quickly.

However, if not enough people are self-scheduling to keep you and your family happily housed, clothed, fed and vacationed, you are going to need to supplement that with some outbound calling. At this point, hopefully, it's not going to be cold-calling, but rather warm-calling. The leads that are coming in from people that are seeing your blog articles, seeing your speeches, reading your book or maybe watching videos that you are posting online, are the people that you are going to want to call first.

From there, there are also a number of other places that you can look for people to call. LinkedIn is particularly useful for business-to-business sales; it is a fantastic tool that allows you to do some highly-targeted searches for people that meet specific criteria who would be good prospects for your business. You can simply reach out to those people online or do a little bit of research and find their business phone number and call them up.

By using the script that you designed, alongside your expert positioning as an author, you should be able to find that you are doing a really good job of scheduling initial conversations with people. Also, prior customers are great to go back to on a regular basis to find out what is going on with them in their business, to see if it's time for you to come back and do some more work for them.

On a semi-regular basis, leads that you may have talked to in the past that did not close are another group of people that you should be making outbound phone calls to. Those people who may not have closed in the past may not have understood your messaging, may not have simply been ready or may not have been in a position to take advantage of your offer at the time. So you do want to follow up with them.

I'm not suggesting that you call them every week, but set up a schedule of something that makes sense to go back through them. Maybe it's once a quarter; maybe it's once every 120 days. As a general rule of thumb, I'd like to get in touch with all of my leads personally every 90 days. Your group of leads may be too big for you to do that, and you can further prioritize them and spread them out a little bit. But do not forget about the people that you've talked to in the past, who may not have closed last time... but may do the next time.

You also should be making a concerted effort to personally contact the people that you do meet at your speaking engagements, at business conferences, at local meet-up events. Even if they did not specifically call attention to the fact that they wanted to schedule time with you, those are definitely leads that you should be reaching out to and attempting to set up conversations or initial appointments with.

Obviously, start with those that have called attention to themselves and said that they do want to have a discussion with you. But as soon as you've gotten through those lists of people, you should be setting aside time on a regular basis to call through your prior customers, to call through your unclosed leads and to call through the other people that you have met at events.

When you spend time writing your book, writing articles and blog posts, posting videos online and doing speaking engagements, you'll find that many more people are proactively seeking you out; or, at the very least, much more willing and desiring to spend that time with you.

I'm often asked, "How do I get my prospects to value my time and my advice?" Proper positioning will fix most of this.

First of all, a lot of what we have discussed along the way definitely will help with that. If you are positioning yourself as an expert, and you're providing value on your calls and on your meetings with people rather than just asking questions that help you but don't really raise any insightful realizations for them, those sorts of things are definitely going to improve your chances that they value your advice.

But the first thing that you end up needing to do on top of that is to start valuing your own time. I often see people, when they're dealing with prospective clients, saying things that give the clients the indication that you have as much time for them as they may need, whenever they need it.

If you say things like you're open at any time; if they miss an appointment or they're late and you tell them that it's no big deal; if every time they call, you pick up on the first ring; if you call them back within five minutes every time that they call you when it is not scheduled; those are all things that give the impression that they are the most important thing that you have going on and that you'll always be available on their time schedule, rather than needing to take care with your time as well.

Instead of positioning yourself that way, you need to make sure that you are setting the mindset both inside yourself and in your clients that you are very busy, that your time is scarce, and that while you're willing to spend time with them, your availability is very limited. One way of doing that – we've touched on this a couple of times – is to schedule your calls with people. Let them know that you're busy; and you want to make sure that you have an opportunity to connect with them. Say, "Let's schedule a time to make sure that we have an opportunity to talk."

Make sure that they know that you have limited availability. When they say, "All right, let's talk next week," don't tell them you're open all week even if that's true. Let them know that you have stuff going on, but it looks like you have availability a couple of times on Tuesday afternoon or perhaps on Wednesday morning. Give them a limited number of times that you're available and try to narrow it down for that.

Then when they come back and say, "Well, actually, I'm going to be out of town from Tuesday through Thursday. Do you have anything on Friday?" You go ahead and either give them limited choices or let them know, "It looks like Friday is going to be okay; it's a little tight. What looks like would be good for you?" And let them give you a time and then decide, "Okay, yeah, I think I can make that work."

Even if your day on Friday is wide open, you want to do the positioning as if you're busy. You'll make it work for them, but now they no longer have the idea that you're just sitting around waiting for them; and it makes it much more likely that they're going to value the time that you're giving them.

It also creates the same air about you that happens if you're walking past two different restaurants. One of them is busy; those inside seem to be having a good time and there are lots of people there and many others waiting. Then there's another restaurant right next door that's completely empty. You're more likely to want to check out the restaurant that's busy, not the one where you can get in right away.

That air of being busy and having demands on your time and the idea that other people are needing and utilizing you is very helpful to your positioning with people. It will ultimately make them value your time more than when you give them the impression that you're available whenever.

The other thing that you want to do is to make sure that when you are talking to your clients, you are providing value to them. As I mentioned, ask good questions. Don't waste their time. Asking questions such as "How many employees do you have?" isn't usually going to be of value to them. You may need to know that in order to put your proposal together for them, but that can usually wait till later in the sales cycle when you're ready to do a proposal.

Alternatively, many times they may want to have someone on their staff spend 15 minutes with you. Ask where you can get some of the situational questions covered so that you've got what you need in order to do the proposal. You want to spend as much time asking insightful questions of them to make them really think about their business and what you can do for them, rather than things where they may be thinking there are other people in the organization that can take care of those details for you.

Also, make sure that every time you're talking to them,

you're offering some advice or some insights or asking questions that really make them think about their business. The customers who feel that they learn something from you every time they talk to you – whether it be because you teach it to them or you make them think about something differently – will promptly return your calls because you're bringing value to them, and they know that talking to you is going to be useful for them. So make sure you're offering insights and advice and bringing value to them on each and every contact.

Ask Powerful Questions

Once you have the first appointment, meeting, or phone call scheduled with your prospect, that's when it's time to really start digging in and learning about your customer. Learn what it is that they need or want, learn about their current situation and learn about what they'd like to see it look like, as well as what it is they see as being the benefits and pay-offs of a change.

The way you're going to do this is through questioning. Asking questions is a major component of the sales system and of critical value to your ability to get their business. When you do questioning wrong, you're going to come across as pushy or salesy. Ultimately, you're going to annoy and turn off your prospects. You're also going to, in some cases, make them see you as being of little value.

If you're not asking questions of them that make you appear different, or that make you appear as if you're really trying to get at the bottom line of how you can improve their business, and not just learn about their specific situation and minor issues; if you're not getting that impression across, they're not going to see the value of wanting to continue to spend time with you and you'll find that your prospects and clients will go dark after this first conversation, and you'll have a much more difficult time getting them on the phone or getting another meeting scheduled.

However, if the questions you ask cause them to think about their business, think about themselves and have insights into themselves and their business, they're going to value the time that they spend with you and be more likely to want to do business with you. So asking great questions is very important.

At the same time, the other thing that you need to do is actually listen to their responses. It's not uncommon for people to ask a question and then completely move on to their next question. It does not give your prospect or client the feeling that you actually really understand them, and it's also entirely possible that you may have slightly misinterpreted what it is that they've said. You want to make sure that you and your prospect are on the same page there.

So every time you ask a prospect a question, and they answer you, you're going to want to repeat back what you've heard. You may not necessarily want to do this for each and every question; you may ask two or three questions in a row, but then repeat back and summarize what you've heard from them. That is how you're going to actually amplify the power of your questions: by making sure that you're responding to exactly what they said and making sure that they know you truly heard them and, more importantly, that you understand them.

Do you even know what you are selling?

It may seem like a silly question, but the reality is that most business owners, coaches, consultants and even professional salespeople that I talk to don't actually know what they're selling. It's critical that the way you talk about your solution or services matches up what the customers think they need.

I often hear business owners talking about what they do by describing what they're selling. They may say, "I'm a chiropractor; I provide chiropractic services," "I cure backaches," "I'm a marketing consultant," "I help companies get more leads," or "I'm a drill salesman." And they say that last one because there's an old sales adage that goes something like: "Don't sell them the drill; you need to sell them the hole."

What that means is that you need to think in terms of the fact that if you've got someone in an aisle of the hardware store, looking at a bunch of drills, they're not really there to buy a drill; yet most of the sales reps that will come up to them in that aisle in their hardware store are going to try to sell them a drill. What they're really there for is that they need to make a hole. Therefore, you should sell them the hole and focus on how easy it will be to make one if you use a particular drill or a particular set of bits versus others, and how clean the hole will be, etc.

That's ultimately what it is that you're selling. I think, though, this approach that misses the mark; and it misses the mark because no one wants a bunch of holes in their wall. That's not really what it is that they're after. You need to dig a little bit deeper. What they may want is that they may want to hang a shelf on the wall where they're going to put pictures of their family from various vacations that they've been on for the last half a dozen years, and they want to ensure that when the cat jumps on that shelf, that the shelf does not fall down and hit their six-month-old child on the head. That's what it is that they really want.

So if you continue with that same sales situation, and you talk about selling a drill, maybe you're going to get a sale for the cheapest drill in that aisle. If you talk about the holes, yes, you'll sell a slightly better drill and probably with a good set of drill bits. But if you come to understand what it is the customer really wants, what it is that you're really selling, then you're going to talk about an additional option, which is the installation service, where you're going to send a guy from the store out to their house with all of the appropriate hardware to make sure that the shelf is put up properly; it's going to be sturdy; it's not going to fall; it's going to be level and straight, so nothing is going to roll off of it.

While you're there, you may have other punch job items that you get to take care for that family as well. You end up with a much more profitable sale. You may need to do this yourself in your business, and it starts from recognizing that every customer has a slightly different take on what they're looking for and what they're buying. Even if the service or product that you offer is the same thing each and every time, each customer has something slightly different that they're looking for from it. It's critical that you understand exactly what that is, before you start pitching.

Here's a great way to do that. I like to ask my favorite three questions early in the sales conversation. I start out my sales conversations by asking a simple question: "Why are you..." and then I fill in whatever it is that they're looking at. So, it could be, "Why are you thinking about marketing training?" If you're in the car business, "Why are you looking at a new car?" "Why are you thinking about training a new team?" "Why are you considering a new copier?" Whatever it is that it seems you're offering, ask them why they're thinking about it. That's usually the first question that I like to ask. When you ask this, you're only beginning to scratch the surface of what's important.

Unfortunately, that's when most salespeople and most business owners will stop. They're asking out of curiosity mostly, and they don't actually even use the information there. You need to learn not to do that. After asking that question, you need to learn from it what they've really come to you for and realize that you haven't really gotten all the way yet; you need to move on.

So then I'll say, "Great. Now what's most important to you about..." and fill in their answer. Thus, after asking "What's most important to you about getting more leads?", you need to listen to what they say, and implement that information. They're going to tell you why they want more leads, and you then take it another step and go a little bit further and ask them, "Okay, so what will *[whatever they tell you]* do for you?"

In the prior example, they're going to tell you, "I need more leads because I'm looking to double the amount of deals that I close in the next year." So what you end up saying is, "Okay, so what will doubling the number of sales in the next year do for you?" Then they're going to tell you, "Well, I'm going to take the increased income and be able to launch a new product line" or "I'm going to take that income because by doubling my sales, I'm going to be able to cover my kid's college."

Whatever it is that they tell you, now it is that you're getting to what it is that they really want, and you need to deliver your pitch and the rest of your conversation with that understanding, and to keep pointing back to what it is that they actually really want. Direct everything you say and relate it back to how it's going to help them get what it is that they really wanted. It's going to set you well beyond any of the other sales reps or businesses that they may be talking to, because you're going to be the only one that comes across as if you understand what it is they want.

So try that formula: ask those questions; practice it; rehearse it, go out and see what kind of difference that makes for you. I think you'll find that very quickly, you're going to end up with customers who are much more eager to do business with you when you change what it is that you're selling.

Don't assume that you know the end result that they want. If someone is coming into a weight loss clinic, don't assume that it is for health reasons; don't assume that it is for vanity reasons; don't assume anything about what it is that they want until they have told you their specific needs and wants.

It's important that you understand not only that they may want to lose weight but also why they want to lose weight and what they think that that is going to do for them. Ultimately, it may be about them feeling attractive; it may be about attracting or keeping someone in their life attracted to them; it may be about getting healthy; it could be about being around for a long time to spend time with their loved ones or their children. There are all sorts of things that may be behind their desire to lose weight.

In the case of a weight loss clinic, if you focus your pitch simply on weight loss and not on what it is that they're ultimately after, you're less likely to turn that prospect into a customer, no matter how great your services may be.

The Four Types of Questions

Present State Questions

Once you've determined their criteria, there are four main types of questions that you're going to want to ask. Ideally, you're going to want to go through these in order. First, you're going to take them through what I call *present state questions*. These present state questions are going to help them describe what's going on now. Questions about present state are going to be things like, "Please tell me about your current situation" or "Can you tell me a little bit about your...?" And it could be your weight loss history; it could be your lead generation; it could be your online marketing.

Obviously, you're going to ask things like: "What is your topic?" or "But can you tell me a little bit about...?" And from that, also go immediately into: "What has worked well for you in the past? What hasn't?" You can ask questions like, "How far from your ideal situation are you now?" These are questions that are focused on what's going on now. At this point, you're not necessarily looking for "Is it a problem?" or how those problems are impacting them, but just simply what the present state is.

Problem State Questions

After you've understood the present state, then you're going to move on to the problem state. So from there, you're going to ask questions that are geared towards getting them to say, "What's wrong with this?" For example:

- What is your greatest challenge in _____??
- What was your greatest disappointment in your _____ last year? Why?
- Why do you feel there is a need for _____ at this time?
- What disadvantages do you foresee in _____?
- If you could change one thing about _____, what would it be?
- What difficulties do you have in _____?
- What will be your primary concern in achieving _____?
- What would be the drawbacks about not _____?
- Are you satisfied with the current _____?
- What is the 1 thing you would like improve about?
- What would you change about?
- What are you doing about _____?

Pacing Questions

From problem questions, you're going to want to move on to pacing questions. What pacing questions are designed to do is to tie their problems into the criteria that you originally got from them, tying back what it is that they've said that their problems are and how that relates to what they really want.

For instance, using a weight loss example, again, you can ask questions like:

- "How is getting and staying healthy going to be

affected if you don't deal with these problems?"

- "What are you missing out on as a result of this?"
- "What do you feel are the consequences for this in your life or in your relationships or in your health?"
- "What effect does all of this have on your ability to stay healthy?"
- "How will you feel about it in one year, five years, or ten years?"
- "How will you feel about this if you haven't made a change in one year, five years, or ten years?"

Tailor your approach to whatever is appropriate, based on the situation.

Pay-off Questions

These are questions that are designed to get them to think about the solution to the problems and what it's going to mean to them when they solve these problems. So sticking with the weight loss example:

- "What do you think you need to do in order to lose the weight in a natural and permanent way?"
- "What would that kind of weight loss accomplish for you?"
- "What's the biggest driving factor that brought you to decide to make this change now?"
- "What will your life or your business be like once

you solve this problem?"

- "What will it enable you to do that you can't do now?"

- "How motivated are you to actually fix this or change this now?"

- "What will it feel like once you've reached your ideal weight?"

- "How do you think it's going to impact the relationships with your friends and family?"

- "How is it going to impact your self-esteem?"

You may notice that in the order of those questions, the last couple of questions are the ones where you're focusing on the positive: "What happens when you actually solve the problem or get the result?" The idea there is that when you're asking pay-off questions, some of them may be depressing or down. So you want to make sure that the last questions you're asking are bringing them back into a positive state.

What specifically should you be asking?

You should also be asking yourself, "Do I know exactly what I need to be asking, and is it written down?"

A lot of people go through their sales process with customers asking mostly the same questions each time, but not always asking everything that's really important. And you need to be asking questions that are insightful and which stimulate conversation with your customers. It's much more important than asking situational-type questions.

We've talked about scripting before, and it's really

important that you script out the questions that you're going to ask your customers and that you choose questions which will get them talking about what is critical in their business. I find that many people spend way too much time asking the wrong questions. For example, some of my least favorite questions that I see salespeople and other professionals asking very early on in the sales cycle are things like:

- "How are you doing?"
- "Tell me about your business?"
- "What's important to you?"
- "Who is your supplier for…?"
- "Do you have a budget?"
- "Do you have a contract in place already?"
- "Who have you been using for…?"
- "How are they treating you?"
- "When is that contract up?"
- "Have you ever heard of us?"
- "What would it take to get your business?"

These are all questions that, particularly early on in the sales cycle, are unimportant. They may be things that are helpful to you, but they're not helpful to your customer; and until you're helpful to your customer, you have very little chance of getting their business. Asking if they have a contract – and if so, how long is left on it – lowers your likelihood of getting business. But I can tell you for certain that your customer having a contract with someone else in many cases does not mean they can't do business with you anyway, along with keeping that contract active.

Thus, it's the wrong question to ask too early, and you're just giving your customer potential excuses not to do business with you and, ultimately, not to see a reason why they should try to find out how they can do business with you. You want to stop with those questions as quickly as possible. You need to focus on questions that are going to get your customers talking about their problems; that's going to get them talking about what solutions they want and get them talking about what's possible in their business when they solve those solutions.

So, I've already shared with you my favorite first three questions to ask people. Here are a few others that I have found incredibly useful and are some of my favorite questions to ask prospects. You can change these questions around so they can fit just about any sort of business. You're going to obviously fill in the blanks in some of these cases; you're going to fill in bits that they've told you when you ask the first three questions that I already taught you, or from what you know from conversation already with them. You can ask them:

- "How has (_) been a problem for you?"
- "What have you found that causes (_)?"
- "What have you experienced in the past when you've tried to change (_)?"
- "What is the worst thing for you about (_)?"
- "What would you say are the top three things that you need to overcome in order to be able to (_)?"
- "What's the impact on you or your business if you don't (_)?"

- "Is there anything that you are missing out on by that?"

- "How does it affect other areas of your life or your business?"

- "What do you think you need to (_) in a comfortable way?"

In that case, the question is going to be: "What do you think you need to change your lead development process in a comfortable way?" Or, "What do you think you need to increase your revenues in a comfortable way?" Whatever the end result they're looking for, that's what you would fill in there. You can also ask, "What are the biggest driving factors that got you to look at making a change now?" Then I'd also like to ask, "What will you do if you can't (_) now?"

There are 10 starting points for questions for you to play around with. As you can see, those are all questions that are trying to get your customer to focus on problems and solutions in their business; how they're going to get there; what it is that they're going to do as a result. Those are the sorts of questions that get your customers thinking, and it helps you get insights into the way that they think, insights into their business, and it gets them associating you with asking high-value questions for them. It's now much more likely that that particular customer is going to want to continue conversations with you and do business with you when they see that you're actually helping them uncover ways of helping their business.

Sometimes, when someone answers your question, you will find that you'd like to know more about what they said. Sometimes, they just don't give you quite enough information, so how do you get them to open up more? It's really pretty simple.

Just ask them to! Try asking these questions to get them to open up or clarify.

- "When you say (_), what exactly does that mean to you?"
- "That's interesting. Tell me a little more about that."
- "When you say (_), how do you mean that exactly?"
- "Can you expand on that a little more for me?"

Pitch, Overcome Objections, and Close

After you have asked your questions (remember, it's a conversation, not an inquisition) of your customer you'll need to transition to presenting your solution. You'll deliver a presentation where you explain the solution that you created and how exactly it solves the problems and challenges that the prospect has expressed. At this stage you'll also detail pricing for them.

Pitch

As you present your solution it's important that you avoid fixating on the features of your solution. Your prospect is looking for "what's in it for me." Most commonly, this will not involve the features of your service very prominently. Instead of features, this is where you'll want to show them the advantages and benefits of your solution.

There is an important distinction to understand here and it's a distinction that most sales training does not take far enough. In case you haven't heard it before, I'm going to explain the difference between *features*, *advantages* and *benefits*.

Features

Features are simply facts, data or information about your product or service. This includes things like

- This car has four wheels and two bucket seats and it is red.

- This phone has 32 GB of memory.

- Your book will give you more exposure.

While you may need to discuss some of the features to explain what the solution is, don't focus too much on it. Your customer is much more concerned with what it will do for them.

Advantages

The next step up from features is advantages. This is what most sales and marketing books and articles will call benefits. Advantages are not really quite benefits, but they are much more important to speak of than features. An advantage shows how a product or service can be used or can help the customer. It is, in essence, an advantage of your product or service. Here are some examples:

- The Maserati Quattroporte can go from 0 to 100 km/h in 4.7 seconds, giving you more thrills than any car you have ever driven before.

- This phone has 32 GB of memory which allows you to store hundreds of photos or videos.

- Your book will give you more exposure, which means more people will hear your message and recognize you as an authority in your field.

Many sales and marketing programs talk about advantages as if they are benefits and just leave it there. You are much better off if you do that than if you focus simply on features... but there is a better way. That better way is to focus as much as possible on true benefits.

Benefits

Take the Maserati from above. If you were trying to sell this car to my son and told him how fast it accelerates and what a thrill he would get from it, you would make no traction with him (excuse the pun). There are a couple reasons for this; one is that he does not like thrill rides. He just doesn't enjoy them. Secondly, and more importantly, he is legally blind. His vision is roughly equivalent to 20/800. He has no depth perception, no peripheral vision and the upper third of a normal field of vision is non-existent to him. The bottom line is that while the acceleration of the car may be an advantage to some, it is really of no benefit to him because he cannot drive.

For an advantage to truly be a benefit, it needs to be a benefit to your prospect, and it should be one that meets **a need or desire the prospect has said he has**, not one that you assume or think they have. It needs to be one they have explicitly expressed. It is part of the reason the questioning phase is so important: You cannot discuss benefits with the customer until you know what they think they need or want.

When you are presenting your solution, try to talk only about as many features as you can tie to an advantage that matches a need they have expressed. Discuss as many benefits with them as possible. That's much more powerful than just showing the advantages. Here are a couple of examples for you:

- This phone has 32 GB or memory so you can store the hundreds of photos and videos of your kids that you said you wanted to have with you all the time.

- Your book will give you more exposure. Not only will more people hear your message, but you'll also be recognized more easily as an expert. That will make it much easier to charge the higher prices that you said you want.

I encourage you to take some time and list out all of the

features of your typical solution and write out several advantages to each. Also, write out several sample benefit statements for them so you get used to phrasing them that way.

Close

Surprisingly, the number one reason that most sales don't close is that most people don't do this one critical thing. This thing is also very easy to do, but seems to be the one thing many fear most: asking for the business.

Very early in my career – in fact, while I was still in college – I got a part-time job working on my college campus selling IBM computer systems to faculty, staff and students. Early on, I wasn't doing all that well; I was doing okay but not great. My manager at the time, and one of my earliest sales mentors, Vince, had taken me aside after listening to several sales conversations that I was having with people.

He told me that the number one thing that I was doing wrong, was simple: I wasn't asking for the business. I was just ending the conversation by letting them say if they were ready to buy or not, without me even implying that it was time for them to do that. As a result, people would walk off. They may have been often ready to buy, but they just needed a very, very slight push at being told, "Okay, now is the time when you can tell me that you want to get the system or not." So he taught me, at the end of every sales conversation, to simply ask for the order.

It wasn't even 30 days later that I had overheard a conversation that one of my friends and a colleague was having with Vince. I only heard a snippet of the conversation, but what I heard was his comment that: "I don't know what it is. All of a sudden, it seems that David is always talking to people, and if I turn my back on them for just a bit, every time I turn around, he's there sitting down, filling out paperwork with them."

It was a fantastic compliment to me about how far I had come, but it had seemed to him that simply just by talking to people, they ultimately ended up filling out paperwork. The only thing that I had changed in my conversations at that point was that I was asking for the order at the end of the call.

The bottom line is that until you ask, the answer is always "no". You typically will not get a "yes"; you will not get a sale until you ask. Even so, most business owners and professionals and, unfortunately, even most professional salespeople, don't ask for the order at the end of every sales call. I hear from people, particularly those that are running their own business, that they are either afraid of asking for the order or they're afraid that they're going to get the "no". The truth is, they already have a "no"; they need to ask if they're going to get a "yes".

Sometimes, people will be afraid that it's going to come up too high pressure; they think that it's going to come across as incongruent; that it just doesn't feel right; that it's awkward to ask for the sale. The truth is that it's awkward for them because they're not used to it yet, but it's actually more awkward for the customer when you don't ask. It's a mindset that you need to get out of. Let me give you an example.

Very early in my dating history, I remember very clearly my first real date; I had worked up the nerve and asked a girl called Jill to come out with me. We went out for dinner and a movie, then we went out for dessert. After the movie, we sat and talked; a very typical 1980s high school date.

We had a really good time; we had fun; we enjoyed the

movie; we had good conversation both at dinner and at dessert afterwards; the conversation flowed really well. We just had a really good time together.

Then the evening came to an end. I drove her home, and being the gentleman that I am, I walked her up to the door... and that is where the evening took a very uncomfortable turn. There was this long pause and neither one of us said anything; Jill was fumbling with her keys; we looked at each other. I tried to come up with things to say to keep the conversation going a little bit while I tried to work up my nerve.

But of course, it was just very incongruent and uncomfortable for both of us. We both knew that the discomfort was over; we both knew what was going to happen next or not happen. But I was too afraid to take the next step, I was too afraid to reach and try to kiss her, just out of the fear that she might not want to.

The end result was that not only did I not get the kiss, but we never ended up going out again. The end of that date was so uncomfortable for both of us as a result of my not asking, of my not taking that next step. It was what was natural; it was what was logical. The worst thing that would have happened is that she would have stopped me and said that she's not ready for that. But because of the way that I went about not doing it, nothing ever happened again.

When you don't ask for the sale at the end of the sales conversation, you are doing the same exact thing. Your prospect knows that you want to know if they're going to do business with you; it's very likely want you to ask. It's when you don't ask that you create a level of discomfort for them, and that discomfort ultimately gets anchored to their feelings for you. It makes the likelihood of getting the sale in a future conversation even worse because now when you call or you email them, they're anchored to that feeling of discomfort... and it's absolutely not what you want.

There's a really simple way to ask for the order that does not come across pushy or salesy. My friend and mentor Ed Rush teaches a very simple way to do it, and it feels great. I've done something very similar throughout my career, but his wording and his suggestion has worked really well for lots of people just like you.

Quite simply, when you're at the end of the conversation and you guys have talked about their problems and you've shown them that you have solutions for that and laid out ways to work together, you just say, "So are you ready to start working together?" That's it, just, "Are you ready to get started working together?" You will get a "yes" much of the time. When you don't get a "yes", you'll usually get a "no".

Most of the times that you get a "no", they will automatically tell you why; they'll say, "No, I'm not ready yet because..." and they will give you a reason. Sometimes, that will be a legitimate reason that will resolve itself; sometimes, that "because" will be simply a starting point for the two of you to start talking. They might say, "No, I'm not ready to do that because it's a little outside of my budget."

Now you can discuss the budget and the services and see if there's somewhere to go with that. Or they'll say, "No, I'm not ready yet because I have 16 projects that I'm working on right now, and I won't have time to focus on this until the beginning of next quarter." Then you can start talking to them about firming things up now and doing planning. So, right at the beginning of next quarter, you guys are going forwards and working together. You may be able to close that sale now, but just schedule it for later.

The bottom line is that until you ask, you won't know what's holding them back from doing business with you, and you won't be in a position to do something about it. Thus, if you want to get more sales, to close more sales, the first thing that you need to do is take a close, hard look at whether you are truly asking every time.

Overcome Objections

After you have presented your solution and asked for the order you also need to be prepared to discuss the prospect's objections with them. Your objective is to help them understand on their own that your solution is what is best for them.

The best time and the best way to overcome your prospect's objection is simply to avoid having them in the first place. Now, of course, you may not be able to foresee all of your prospects objections, but it's likely that you get the same ones frequently. If there is a recurring problem with your product or service or a simple misunderstanding about your product or service, or a common misconception that some prospects have, you should deal with it right away. Don't try to gloss over it or hide it. The best thing to do is bring it up on your own.

Bringing the problem up yourself makes it easier to handle and ensures that you're not on the defensive. You can apply the strategy almost anywhere in the sales process where you expect an objection may come up. If your experience tells you that there is a real possibility of the customer raising an objection, you should learn to deal with it proactively.

An important point here, though, is that it must be something your experience has told you your customers bring up.

Do not assume that what you think may be an objection is one your customers have. It's important not to project your insecurities about your product or solution onto your customers. Deal with the objections they bring up.

A great starting point for preparing to deal with objections is to know what all the objections you get are. To do that take a few minutes and write down every objection that you can remember getting about your product and service. This will serve as a great guide, and you will want to take the time to write out responses to each of these. For the most common ones, you'll not only want a response for when a customer brings it up, but you'll want to script out the language you use to proactively hand off the objection.

Understanding Objections

In order to best be able to handle and overcome objections, you will want to understand the four types of objections, and to implement a simple seven-step process to overcoming them.

It is helpful, as you are working on your objection-handling scripts, to understand the four types of sales objections:

- **Lack of Need.** This is the most basic objection. Your prospect needs to feel that they need what you are offering.

- **Lack of Urgency.** They may need what you are offering but don't have the sense of urgency to solve the problem now.

- **Lack of Money.** This common objection can either be true (and uncovered in the questioning phase) or simply an attempt to get you to lower your price

- **Lack of Trust.** This objection boils down to the prospect believing that you can do what you say you can do for them.

Lack of need objections come up because you did not spend enough time in the questioning phase making sure that you have properly established that a) they feel they have a need and b) they need or want to solve it. Again, it is critical that you let your prospect state they have a need; don't assume it and don't project the need on them.

Sometimes, these sorts of objections will come up when you are focused on the pitch and presentation of the process or features of your solution, rather than on the outcome. If your customer has expressed an explicit need, and yet thinks they don't need your solution, this is most likely the case. Back up and make sure that you ask some additional questions to dig deeper into the problems they expressed. Make sure that you are discussing with them the outcome they will get from your solution.

Lack of urgency is also usually something that could and should be discovered in the questioning phase. Make sure that you have them determine and express how important solving the problem is, and their timeline for doing so.

If your prospect has agreed that the problem is urgent and needs to be solved quickly, yet they still don't feel urgency about your proposal, it is likely that you have not demonstrated the impact of your solution well enough for them. If they still have the need, go back and help them to see the impact that you can have, and show them how you can help.

To do that, you'll want to focus on two things. First, you'll need to demonstrate the *logical impact* of the solution. That is the details of the business case and return on investment (ROI) of your solution. People do not make decisions just on the logic of a solution, though. You'll need to also appeal to their heart by demonstrating the *emotional impact* of the solution. Of the two, the heart is often more important. To overcome a lack of emotional urgency, you'll need to focus with the prospect on the emotional drivers of the problem, and how you can go about solving it. Make sure that you focus with them on what they want to ultimately achieve beyond just solving the obvious problem. Part of the reason that we ask "What will that do for you?" two or three times at the beginning of the questioning phase is to get past the basics of their problem.

Some good questions to ask here are:

- If you are able to do this, what will that do for your (_)?

- If you were able to work on this and get this done, what will happen to your goals?

- If you delay, or don't act, what consequences might you face?

To deal with a **lack of money** objection, first you must listen fully and confirm if money is really the issue. Often, money objections are raised as a cover for something else. Work to fully uncover the real objection. Try asking, "If money were no object, what would your ideal solution be?" If you and the prospect have a common or similar vision, it's easier to deal with. If you don't have a common vision of an ideal solution, or your solution contradicts their ideal, you'll have a harder time with this objection.

Sometimes, they will want you to break down the details of your cost structure and your hourly rates. I recommend that you do not go down the path of talking about cost structure. Often, a prospect will ask you to break down the pricing into billable hours so they can understand it better. It's a slippery slope that will have you justifying your price and not your value.

If their objection is that the total price is too high, one way of dealing with that is to offer to reduce the scope of the work done to lower the cost. Ask them what part of the project they want to drop. That way, you don't risk making them think that your price was arbitrary when you suddenly can lower it.

The final type of objection is **lack of trust**. They either do not believe you or that you can do what you say you can do for them. The number one cause of this is that you did not seem genuine to them or that they did not feel you showed sincere interest in them or their problem. Remember, you are having a conversation with a person. Interact with them that way. Treating them like a number, a burden, or without emotion, will inevitably lower trust.

Having a bestselling book, a blog with lots of content that teaches instead of tries to sell or online videos is a great way of building likeability, trust and rapport with them before you ever even meet and get to the presentation stage. Once the objection comes up, though, the first thing you need to do is ask more questions of them. Asking insightful questions is one of the best ways of building rapport. Don't ask questions designed to corner them. That only will hurt trust. Ask questions that make them think. Then transition back into talking about your solution; relate a success story where you've helped a similar business or someone with a similar challenge.

The seven-step process for overcoming objections is as follows:

1. **Remain silent.**

2. **Gather information.**

3. **Understand.**

4. **Confirm.**

5. **Handle.**

6. **Check for customer satisfaction.**

7. **Ask for the order.**

The first step is to **remain silent**. When a customer expresses an objection, don't immediately jump in to try to answer. Taking a moment to stay silent gives you time to think – as well as giving them time to think. You may find that they even answer their own question or overcome the objection on their own. Another reason for staying silent is that they may not actually be done talking. If they perceive you are interrupting them, they may feel as if you are objecting to them objecting. If you make them feel that you are not listening to them you will lose the opportunity.

It's entirely possible that when you give them a little bit of time and silence that they'll solve the problem on their own. Have you ever had an experience where you started to ask someone a question and as you were verbalizing it and explaining it to them, the answer or solution became immediately obvious to you? Just as a customer need is most powerful if they express it, so is the answer to their own question or objection. Sometimes, they just need to verbalize it in order to realize that their objection really isn't one, or may not matter. Use silence to give them that opportunity.

Next, you'll want to **gather information**. Before launching into an answer to the question or into your script for handling that particular objection, you'll want to ask appropriate questions to make sure you understand what they truly meant.

There are two great questions to ask to help gather information at this point. The first question I like to ask is, "Tell me more about..." The other is, "What do you mean by...?" Both of those questions are great at getting customers to open up about their objection.

One thing you should not ask at this point is any question that begins with why. Asking why will get your customer to express and reinforce to themselves the objection that they have. You simply want to gather information, not help them confirm that their objection is valid.

Once you have gathered enough information about their objection, you'll want to make sure that you understand, and, crucially, that they feel that you understand. In the book *The Seven Habits of Highly Effective People*, Stephen Covey cited one of the habits as: "Seek first to understand, then to be understood." In order to overcome or handle an objection in a productive and collaborative way with your prospect, you must create an atmosphere of caring, positive problem solving and trust. To do that, your prospect must know you understand them. Plus, in order for you to properly solve the objection, you need to actually understand what the prospect means. It does you no good to overcome an objection different than what the customer meant.

Then, **confirm** that solving the proffered objection will actually move the sale forwards. There is very little that is more frustrating than to brilliantly handle a customer objection only to discover that it was a smoke screen for something else entirely. A simple way to do this is, once again, to simply ask. For example, "If I could guarantee you that we can get the project done by your deadline, will you be ready to move forwards today?" If your prospect says yes, then great; it's time to deal with the objection. If they say no, however, you need to step back into gathering information to find out what the additional (or real) objection is.

To **handle** or overcome the objection, you need to provide the customer with the necessary information to eliminate the objection or render it irrelevant. The best way to do that is to be prepared. Know ahead of time exactly how to discuss your most common objections.

After handling the objection, do not assume that your flawless presentation of your objection-handling script has made them think their objection has been handled or that they are ready to move forwards. You'll need to **check for customer satisfaction**, by confirming that they feel the objection has been handled. To do that, simply ask them, "Does this make more sense now?" or "Have I handled this to your satisfaction?"

Provided they say yes, then it's time to either move on to any additional objections you have uncovered, or once again, **ask for the order**.

Follow Up

A critical step in any sales system is follow-up. There are many reasons and places you will need to follow up with prospects and customers, so unlike the other steps, follow-up does not come in any particular order. Instead, it is really part of every other step.

There are three major types of follow-up that you'll need to do with prospects and customers: (1) to move a sale forwards, (2) to ask for more business and expand your relationship with your customer, and (3) to ask for referrals. You may notice that two of the three types of follow-up take place after the sale. In fact, there is another type of after-sale follow-up that I'll recommend as well, and that's (4) to express gratitude.

It's not uncommon to see some people get in mindless follow-up loops with prospects that seem interested, but then the deal never seems to happen or move forwards.

Assuming that the client was genuinely interested in what you had to offer and has the money for your solution, these are things that, as we previously talked about, you should be confirming early in the sales cycle. If that's really the case, the simplest way to clear this problem from happening in the future is to make sure that you were really focusing on scheduling the next call or the next meeting before you adjourned the current meeting or call.

I see a lot of times where sales meetings end, but for whatever reason didn't end in closing of the sale, and the sales process is continuing. I see a lot of those meetings end with, "Okay, let's talk next week;" "Let's talk next month;" "Let's talk again at the beginning of the quarter," or whatever it is, but there's some nebulous discussion of continuing the sales conversation without specifically scheduling it. This is perhaps the single biggest mistake that you can make when a meeting does not end in a sale.

In this day and age, it has become more and more difficult to get a hold of people directly. As such, it's really important that any time you're continuing your sales conversation with the prospect, you schedule a specific date and time to talk or meet. When you're leaving that meeting, and you end up saying that you're going to talk next week, you're going to talk in a month, or whatever it is, make sure that you say: "So that we don't end up missing each other and ending up in phone tag, let's take a look at our calendars real quickly and decide when we'll get back in touch."

Then pull out your calendar and make a suggestion. If they say, "...in about a week," what I frequently end up doing is say, "Okay, how does this same time work next Wednesday?" or whatever day it is, and I'll make a suggestion. Don't give them a choice of suggestions at this point. Just make one particular suggestion that you know works for you and see where they go from there.

Oftentimes, they'll just say, "Okay, that works," and then you schedule it, and you're done. Or that may not work, and then you just start looking and trying to figure out what does actually end up working. Oftentimes, clients actually do have the best intention of talking to you next week... but then things come up. And since you didn't actually schedule something, you just end up later not having the availability. The easiest way to clear it up is just make sure that it's scheduled; that way, you're on their calendar, and it's a priority.

Another thing that I'd like to do is that I send an LOU. No, I'm not talking about the Incredible Hulk Lou right now. I'm talking about a very simple email template that I use. I refer to it as the *Letter of Understanding*, or *LOU*. It's very simple. What I like to do after an in-depth sales conversation is to outline what we discussed about the key points. In particular, I outline the challenges or problems that the client said they had, reiterate that they said they wanted to fix it, and just do a brief overview. The email will essentially say, "Hey, it was great meeting with you today," or "Great talking to you today. Just to recap, here's what I had in the notes from our meeting," and put together that recap. And then I write, "Please let me know if there's anything significant that you think I missed or you want to make sure we talk about next time."

Then I follow up and say, "I look forwards to speaking with you [or seeing you] again on..." and then reiterate the date and time that you scheduled that next appointment for. Then what you want to do is say, "In the meantime, before that meeting, I will be doing X, Y, and Z" or whatever it is that you committed to doing in between now and the next meeting. "And you said that you would be doing X" and put in whatever it is they said they would do.

After you schedule a date and time for the next meeting, it's really helpful to make sure that you are taking some active responsibility of something you'll do before the next meeting and that you're having them do something. It may be an internal meeting; it may be that they're pulling some internal numbers for you; it may be that they're talking to their banker or trying to figure out financing.

Whatever it is that they're going to do, their taking action and committing to doing something is a great sign that they're actually engaged in moving this out forwards. If they won't commit to actually doing something, then it's a sign that they're not really invested in the process and not really all that into the solution that you are talking about.

I like to send out that email typically within 24 hours of the end of that conversation. Oftentimes, I find it gets done from me; it gets done most likely if I do it right away. But whenever you choose to do it, make sure you get those out quickly. It's a great habit to get into. It reiterates and makes sure it reminds the prospect when your appointment is and what their commitments are and puts a reminder in front of them.

When they're looking at their calendar and saying, "Okay, I'm meeting with David on Wednesday. I don't really remember what it was that we were meeting about or why was this important," it outlines for them why they said it was important, what it is you'll be discussing, when it is and what they need to do. It's a great way of increasing the likelihood that those next phone calls or meetings will happen as scheduled.

Another time I see this happen very frequently for customers is when they're sending out a proposal. After a great sales conversation or maybe several sales conversations, the client finally asks for a proposal, and you go ahead and send the proposal off, and that's certainly when you start having difficulty hearing from them. That usually ends up happening because they have a pricing issue or you're missing something from the solution that they thought was important; something about your proposal just didn't strike them right, and suddenly, you've lost some level of rapport, and you've lost some level of prioritization in their eyes for it.

A great way of avoiding that happening is to make sure that you are never just blindly sending a proposal through. First of all, you should always be confirming before the proposal what the next steps are and, once you make the proposal, what's the next thing that happens. Find out from them what their budget is; or, a great question to ask is, "Based on what we've discussed needs to be done, how much are you hoping this will work out to?"

If they don't yet have a budget, that's a great way of getting a number from them. What they're hoping for is something that seems very low risk for them to answer and frequently, they'll say something like: "Okay, now Dave, I'm hoping that it's going to be in the $5,000 to $7,000 range." Then you know immediately that if you're going to be in the $20,000 to $30,000, you need to have a discussion right then and there about how to get back down into their range or how to get them to increase what they're willing and able to spend on it.

First of all, you're confirming that they have acknowledged the problem; that they want to resolve it; what they're going to do next once they get the proposal; what sort of money they're thinking this is going to end up running; you're confirming all that stuff before sending the proposal.

The next thing that you want to do is figure out how long it's going to take you to get the proposal together, agree on a timeline with them of when you're going to get the proposal to them, and then schedule a call or meeting to review the proposal with them. Let them know that you've put the proposal together: "What I'd like to do is schedule some time next Tuesday at 4pm" or whatever time you want to suggest to go through the proposal. Make sure that everything you want to include is in there.

Then once you schedule that meeting, don't send the proposal to them. If you're not going to be reviewing with them in person, then it should be sent to them by email as you are starting that phone call. That way, you have an opportunity to hear their reaction when they see the pricing, when they see what the products and services are. If they have some hesitation or challenge or question about it, you are right there at the moment that they're seeing it. Rather than letting it sink in for hours, days or even weeks that the pricing is out of whack from what they had previously assumed, you want to ideally be able to deal with it immediately.

Most of the time, when you set it up front with clients that way and they know that you guys will be reviewing the proposal together, they're usually very amenable to it. Then you can just go ahead and schedule it – and you send that email as you are making that call.

When you make your follow-up call, you'll want to avoid sounding like every other sales rep that they've spoken with. You do this by avoiding some of the common openers that average reps use when following up. Avoid statements like, "I was calling to follow up...", "I am calling to see if you had any questions", "I just wanted to make sure you got my email (or proposal)", or "The reason for my call was to see if you had come to a decision". Also, avoid saying: "I'm just calling to touch base". These things will not make you stand out as someone they want to work with; it will just lump you in with every other sales rep they've ever met.

Instead, use an opening statement that sets you apart. Construct your opening this way:

1. Introduce yourself using your full name and company name.

2. Remind them why you are calling. Use the pain, gain or need that they expressed they wanted. That's what you are calling about, not touching base.

3. Recommend your next step or an agenda.

For example, "This is David Traub from Sell Brilliantly. Pete, when we spoke last week, you were concerned about the low percentage of your prospects that were turning into customers, and you said you felt you needed to bring more leads into your pipeline. What I'd like to recommend as we continue our conversation is to first explore your lead acquisition process to look for ways to improve, and then to review how you currently convert your leads into sales. Then we can determine the next steps if applicable. How does that sound? Is there anything else you want to cover?"

After you have sold a client, there are three key types of follow-up that you should do with them.

Three Types of Follow-Up after a Sale

First of all, express your gratitude that they are your customer and thank them. I can't say enough how important it is to get into a regular thank you note habit. It is one of the most effective ways you can improve your sales process.

When you send a note to someone it shows that you respect the person and is a concrete way of expressing your appreciation. I want to caution you that I am referring to an actual thank you note, NOT an email. You should send thank you notes when you close a sale (at the very least), and preferably again after someone gives you a referral.

Many top sales reps also send a note after setting an appointment by phone, after an appointment regardless of whether the prospect purchased or not and on the anniversary date of a customer's first deal.

When you take the time to sincerely thank someone for their business or their time, you set yourself apart from the pack. You reinforce that you are someone to like and trust.

Some people will send something on a personalized note paper, others will send a card. I particularly like to send cards. To make that process less time-consuming, I use an online service to send the card. They have hundreds of card selections and even allow you to upload photos to design your own. You can even have them convert your handwriting and signature to a font so what you send is in your own hand. I love using this service. As a special gift to you for reading my book, I've arranged for you to be able to send a card free of charge to someone you care about and see how easy it is and how it makes them feel. Simply go to bonus.TeamOfOneBook.com/card

You should also have a regular schedule with which you contact prior clients to ask for referrals and to explore additional business with them. Your existing customer base is often your best lead source. Set a schedule to contact old customers every 90 to 120 days after your deal is closed for this purpose.

I hear from a lot of customers that a common challenge they face is that when they have follow-up calls with prospects, those calls oftentimes end without them feeling like the sale has moved any further along. Oftentimes, they say that they'll turn into general Q&A sessions; and while they may accomplish a lot on that call, once it's done, there doesn't seem to be any additional movement forwards.

When that happens, it's often because the meeting or the call itself, was not properly planned. One of the key concepts throughout the sales cycle that you need to keep in mind is that you should plan ahead of time for each call and for each meeting. A great way to do this is to first sit down and understand what your intention for the upcoming meeting or phone call is.

Also, make sure that you then build an agenda for the meeting. The agenda doesn't have to be a long, complicated thing; you may be having what's only going to be a 10 or 15 minute phone call. But have a clearly defined purpose for what the call is about; have the two or three or however many points of things that you want to cover on the call in order planned out for the discussion.

Also, plan out at the end how you want to actually close out that discussion; are you asking for the business? Are you asking for something else to happen that needs to take place along the way; maybe an introduction to another party or maybe it's that you guys will do a pilot program. Whatever it is, decide up-front what it is that you think that you should be asking for at the end of the call.

Secondly, once you've come up with your own intention for that call and plan, either the day before, a couple of days before or a week before, depending on what you feel is appropriate based on the scope of the meeting, go ahead and put that agenda in writing in a very simple email that you will send to the person you're having the meeting with, and send it to them as a reminder. It can be very simple and say, "Hey, in light of our meeting coming up tomorrow or next week, I wanted to send out what my thoughts for the agenda are. Here's what I think we should cover," and then outline points A, B, C and D.

It may be a review of details of the proposal, followed by a discussion of how you're going to measure success along the way. Item three may be talking about the scope of the marketing tied to the project. Then item four would be something along the lines of finalizing contract terms, or it could be deciding the next steps in order to make such and such project (whatever it is you're calling the project) start on time by such and such date (whatever the timeline is that you want to try to help the project start). Lay out near the end of the agenda that you're going to be discussing next steps or that you are going to be deciding on finalizing the contract.

Then right at the very end of the agenda, put a quick note in there saying, "Is there anything else you think is important to cover on the call [or in the meeting]?" That way, it gives the person not only a reminder on your agenda but lets you know ahead of time if they've got other things that they're going to throw into it that you may not have planned for. So rather than you being caught off-guard, now you have an opportunity of knowing ahead of time that they also want to discuss budget or they may want to discuss how to get costs down or whatever it is that's going to be added to it; you can know going into the meeting that that's going to happen.

That will lessen the likelihood that because of the call or meeting, you leave there with follow-up tasks that really just stall the whole thing. Instead, you'll be able to go into that meeting with a plan of how to accomplish or discuss whatever it is that they now wanted to add to the agenda. That would be the way of getting the agenda to the customer; of making sure that it is sent out ahead of time.

Additionally, when you start that call or meeting, it's great to start with the agenda. You just let them know, "Before we get going, real quickly, I just want to make sure that we're on the same page here. Just to recap, here's the agenda that I have sent over to you; here's how I think we should approach this meeting. You also said you wanted to discuss..." and then add into the agenda whatever the agenda items that they may have sent to you. "Then at the end of this call or end of this meeting, I'd like to make sure that we discuss and finalize..."

You may say here, if it's appropriate, that you're going to ask for the business. So, "At the end of the meeting, I'd like to make sure that we come to a decision together of whether we're going to be able to work together." Alternatively, if the outcome of the meeting is some other step, then just let them know: "I'd like to make sure at the end of the meeting that we decide on how to move forwards for..." i.e. whatever that next step it is that you want to be scheduling, the presentation to the board or whatever it is that may come next.

But make sure that you outline at the beginning of the meeting what it is that you're intending to discuss and ask for at the end. This way, you'll both be aware of it going into that meeting, and they're not shocked and surprised at the end when you ask your closing questions; whether it be that you're trying to close the business or just simply close to the next step.

Approaching it in this manner will make for a very smooth meeting. Also, make sure that everybody is deciding up-front that at the end of the meeting, you're making some sort of decision. That really helps in making sure that everything is moving forwards with the opportunity and with the deal.

Bonus: The Questions Report

Asking powerful questions may be the most important thing you can do to improve your sales success. Text **#QUESTIONS** to (847) 380-8117 and I'll send my special Questions Report that will help you build your questioning arsenal and ensure you are asking questions that get your prospects thinking and buying.

Common Questions and Pitfalls

How do I get more appointments?

One common question that I get is, "How do I get or book more appointments?" The number one reason why people are not scheduling enough appointments with prospective clients is that when they're talking to potential clients about scheduling the appointment, they are going way past what's necessary.

It's really important to remember that in every part of a system, you need to go one step at a time. When you are at the point in the sales cycle of simply having a meeting with a client, that's all that you need to focus on selling; just selling the appointment. It's very common to want to tell as much as possible about your products or your services and benefits that you offer to customers all on that first call, and then end up asking for the sale.

But what happens in this scenario is that until a potential customer truly knows, likes and trusts you, if you are talking to them and trying to schedule an appointment, they will simply be looking for a reason to not spend time with you. They have tons of things to spend their time on and they are looking for reasons to filter you out.

The more you say on that first call or in that first conversation, the higher the chances that you are telling them something that they may not like or may not agree with. Thus, you instantly become just another person that they don't want to spend time with. Regardless of your approach or how correct what you said to them might be, you won't have an opportunity to explain it to them or show it to them or get them to see what is really going to help their business. Again, what you want to do is not sell your whole service; you're just selling the benefits of sitting down and having a meeting.

A number of years ago, I was leading a sales team. When I

came on board, one of the folks on that team was called Matt and he was not living up to anywhere near what his overall potential was. He was very personable; a really great guy; he had the potential to become a really great sales rep... but he just wasn't getting the results. When we took a look at his sales pipeline, the biggest hole that he had was that he wasn't having enough appointments. Appointments are, quite simply, what is needed to turn those potential opportunities into sales and ultimately close those new deals.

When I listened to him trying to schedule appointments, what I found (as many people do when they're selling) is that he would give all the information that he could on that first call. He was essentially overwhelming the prospect by saying so much, believing that the more he told them, the more convinced to set up the appointment they would be; when actually, the opposite is true. The more you give them on that first call, the more likely it is that they won't want to meet with you.

What we ended up doing was refocusing on his first call to customers. At this point, in his case, they were actual, true cold-calls. He was calling from of a list of people who had never requested information, who didn't necessarily even know who the company was. They were very raw cold-calls. We focused on that first call to make the call as simple and succinct as possible. He used a very strong opener and gave people just a tease of what the benefits were that could be gotten from working with us. Then he would go on to ask if it they were interested in having a discussion about how those benefits could help their company; just a very simple pitch for the appointment, not a pitch for the business.

That had such an impact on his business that just 90 days later, he was on his way to a promotion. Another 120 days later, he was sending me an email with a picture of the house that he was suddenly able to buy because of the dramatic impact that it had on his business.

Thus, what I'd recommend that you do, is to make sure that on your initial call with someone when you're trying to schedule an appointment, that you are offering value to them in ways of talking about what are the benefits of your service. Focus just on the end results that could be gotten from working with you and on finding out if that is something that is of interest to them. But don't try to teach or explain how you do all of that. Just focus on what those benefits are. Be succinct; ask questions of them that make them think about their business and think about the results they're getting and what could be different or better.

But don't waste their time asking a ton of questions that at this stage don't really mean a lot. By that, I mean hear a lot of people on first calls asking: "Do you have a contract for such and such?" "Do you have budget for this?" "When is your contract up?" Have you ever heard of us?" These are things that at this stage aren't going to impact whether you ultimately get the business and establish value with the customer or not. More often than not, people focus on those things when ultimately, all of those situations can be dealt with later in the sales cycle once the customer has reason to want to do business with you.

You also should script out what it is that you are going to say. You need to be as succinct as possible and you need to test and see what is working and what is resonating with customers. You can only do that if you track what it is you're going to say. So take a few minutes and go ahead and write out what your opener on a call should be when you're calling both a warm lead and a cold lead.

Plan out how you're going to ask for the appointment, and then go back through what you've written and look for every conceivable word that you can get rid of and still make the same point. Make sure that you have something in there that is providing benefits to the people; you want to focus on talking about the value that you bring to their company and other companies – and nothing else.

Bonus: Great call openers

I have examples of some great openers for those potential calls. If you'd like to see those text **#OPENERS** to (847) 380-8117 and I'll send you my guide to opening sales calls that get results.

Should I leave a voicemail?

Another common question that I get is, "When I'm making prospecting calls, should I leave a voicemail?" And my answer to this is a resounding yes! When you're making prospecting calls, you absolutely should leave a voicemail message.

Now, there's nothing wrong with making two or three attempts in a day or over a couple days to the same prospect before leaving a message, but you absolutely should be leaving a message when you are prospecting.

You may wonder why so many voicemails fail (by fail, I mean that you don't get a return phone call, and when you call again the person doesn't have any idea or recollection that you called). The number one reason is that the sales person isn't prepared to leave a quality message before picking up the phone. You need to have a voicemail planned out, so that you know ahead of time what you're going to say when you get to someone's voicemail, and you are able to leave a killer voicemail message for them.

The second reason that many voicemails fail is that the person leaving it has no understanding of how to leave a compelling message, which includes a reason for a call back.

You won't always get a return phone call; but oftentimes, the fact that you're trying to get hold of the person alone will be enough for them to want to learn who you are and understand your message. This way, when you call back, they're more likely to take your call. You'll want to build a script for this voicemail. It will be short and to the point, and you'll want to start with the hot button issues that your product or your solution solves.

That's what you want to leave for them. You need to know why your best clients are your best clients; what are the problems that you have solved for them (and not from your perspective, but from theirs); what it is that you did for them; and finally, to make sure that the material you're using is, in fact, what your clients have told you are the reasons that they did business with you.

Here's an example for you: "Hi, this is David from Sell Brilliantly. I'm calling today because we help coaches, consultants and independent professionals such as yourself get the sales results in their business of a full-time sales team, without actually having one. Our last three clients actually doubled their sales in less than 90 days. I'm calling to see if this process would work for you. You can reach me at..." then you leave your phone number. "Again, this is David Traub at..." and you leave your phone number.

If you are calling someone you already have met, you can change it up and try something like this "Hi, this is David from Sell Brilliantly. I am calling because I was thinking about your business and I have an idea I'd like to share with you that I think will help you... [fill in a hot button you know they have]. Call me back at XXX-XXX-XXXX and I'll let you know what I came up with for you."

If you are calling from a referral then try "Hi, this is David from Sell Brilliantly. I was just speaking with... [name who gave you the referral] and he/she mentioned I should give you a call to get your feedback on something. I can be reached at ...."

Those simple messages, or something very much like it, have worked repeatedly for me and many other top sales professionals over the years. So take that message and model it around your business. The next thing to know is that when you leave a voicemail message for someone, send them an email as well. In this day and age, it's usually pretty easy to get people's email addresses even if you've not spoken with them. However, spend just a little bit of time. Don't obsess over it; don't spend hours researching all these people's email addresses. But when you leave a voicemail message for someone, try to find their email address – oftentimes, you may already have it – and send essentially the same message to them in email. You don't know yet whether your customer prefers to talk, meet in person, text message or send an email.

Having this email ready to go and send out to them will very frequently get a response to the email saying, "Hey, I'd love to talk to you, but I'm out of town until next week. Can we talk on Tuesday?" or something to that effect. You'll find out very quickly that some people will raise their hand more quickly through the email. So send both. I like using an email subject of simply "Voicemail" or "I just left you a voicemail." Both get great responses.

Also, you should have more than one of those scripts ready to go. You want to have a different mix of solutions that you're talking about. When you call someone the first time, maybe you left the message and that didn't hit their hot buttons. They may not have called or emailed you back because that wasn't what they needed; so the next time, you're going to leave a slightly different message and you're going to push different hot buttons. Then the same thing on call number three.

Each time, leave slightly different hot buttons. I would highly suggest, so you don't get yourself confused, that you leave the same order every time. The first time you leave a voicemail for a prospect, leave message 1, then move onto message 2, then move onto message 3. That way, you're opening yourself up to different potential results to try to get people's attention each time.

Also, before you start leaving these new voicemails, practice them. Say them out loud several times. If possible, record yourself and listen to the playback. The more you practice, the more prepared you will be... and the better results you will get.

Furthermore, I highly recommend that you try to leverage technology here to work in your favor. One great way of doing that is in the email that you send to these people. Give them an easy way to schedule a quick 10 to 15 minute phone call with you to discuss further if they're interested. There are a number of tools that you can use to do this.

At the end of this chapter, I will list out two or three that you can take a look at; I should note, though, that I use a program called TimeTrade in order to do this. I always put at the end of the email something like: "If you'd like to schedule a time so that we can discuss this, you can use the link below, and you'll see my schedule and availability in real time," and then I'll put the link.

Not a week goes by that I don't come into the week with several calls scheduled with people that I've not spoken with yet (but they got my initial message), who were interested in what I had to say and then scheduled a time on their own. There's no phone tag anymore; there's no hoping that I'm going to get them at a particular date and time; they've picked a time, they've given me a phone number to call... and it does wonders for you when you give people the ability to schedule a time for your own initial call with them. I highly encourage you to take advantage of a tool like that.

How can I more effectively use email?

With the increasing importance of email in all of our communications, one thing that more people should look at is how to effectively use email in their sales.

First of all, I see a lot of people using it to send quick questions to their customers; to sometimes send longer questions or diatribes to their customers in place of picking up the phone and having a conversation with them. It's important to remember that when it comes to selling, email should not be a replacement for talking to your customers.

You may be able to write some great email copy; you may be able to drive a significant traffic to your marketing funnels through email; you may even be able to sell through email. But it will never be as effective as having a conversation with a prospective customer. So make sure that you are not trying to have what should be a conversation through email.

That being said, email is a highly effective way of getting a hold of your customers, getting information to them and getting details from them as well. It can help drive traffic, it can help get deals unstuck and it can help cut down on phone tag. One thing to keep in mind is that everybody gets way too much email, so when you do send an email, please make sure to keep it as brief as possible. Use no more words than necessary to get your point or question across.

It also should be used when you send a voicemail – we already touched on this when we talked about voicemail messages. But since it's often easier for people to reply to an email than to a voicemail, it's ideal when you send a voicemail to also send an email. Sometimes, you may have more information to impart than is feasible in the voicemail, so your voicemail can refer to the fact that you're sending an email as well.

Even if you are saying the exact same thing on voicemail and in the email, you'll want to do both. That way you are covering your bases, no matter whichever is easier or best for your customer to reply to. When you give people multiple channels and multiple options of how to respond to your message, it's definitely going to increase the response rates that you get from your voicemails.

Also, don't forget to use LOU. We talked about this as well earlier, but sending *letters of understanding* is a very effective way of making sure that you're documenting your sales messages with your customers. Also, they're great in situations where the person you're selling to needs to share details with others. It gives them a great way of making sure that all of the key points are being shared with others in the organization as well, and it allows you to make sure that they don't leave something important out.

When you have customers or prospects that have not been responding or have been in your pipeline for a while, email can also be a great way of either moving them along or moving them out of your pipeline and finally getting an answer and understanding of what's going on.

There's a nine-word email that I use frequently and that I get tremendous response from; that email really just goes like this. Firstly, there's a two-word subject line; it just simply says, "Are you..." Then, in the body of the email, I say, "Still interested in..." and then the benefit that we had been discussing, punctuated with a question mark. Then I sign it. My preferred signature is "All the best, David," and my contact information.

But that email is a great option when you've been trying to get hold of a prospect after having discussions with them, and they've just gone silent or dark on you. It's short; it's to the point; and frequently, people who didn't have the time or hadn't taken the step of returning your call or prior emails will reply. You may get a short email that just simply says, "Yes, can't act on it till next month." Or they may write back and say, "No, not at this time."

If you get a "no", you can obviously try to get hold of them or reply and ask to see if you can get more details. Oftentimes, they'll give you what the details are, and then you have an objection to try to start working with and see if there's a way of dealing with it. But the "Are you…" email has been one of the most effective emails that I've had in my arsenal for years in order to kick-start stuck deals and get them unstuck.

That relates very well to my next point here: one of the reasons why with that email I get such high response rates, is that the subject line is part of a sentence. It starts to ask a question… and then drops off in the middle. The beginning of a question as your email subject line can be very effective in getting people to reply and actually read your emails.

Sometimes, when we send emails to our customers – even when they're not to a mailing list but simply a very specific email to a specific person – they don't get read. Obviously, the subject line is an important part of that, because it helps people sort through the emails in their inbox quickly.

Sometimes, though, the subject line on its own is able to summarize for them what the email is going to be about, which, by rights, it should. However, in these cases, you'll sometimes find that people will leave it unread or leave it for later because they know that they want to read it and take a look at it… and then it just gets buried under the rest of their email and they have a hard time finding it later.

But there's something about asking a question. When you ask question, people naturally want their brains to want to answer it. But worse than that (or for us, better than that) is the fact that they don't like part of something. So when you ask something that's incomplete in your subject line, it's almost compelling them to open it up and read at least the first sentence of the email message. Then, once they're there, they usually read the whole thing. So, "Are you…" falls into that category.

You can use any question in that subject line; just make sure that you drop it off before they know what the whole question is. It drives them to read the rest of it. You can ask "When can we…" or "Will you be able to…" Things like have a great response rate of people opening them.

However, for that to work, it's important that you don't do that just to get people to open the email, and then start your message with something completely unrelated. You need to finish that question; and it should be a question that they could send you a quick and simple answer to. So you don't want to deceive them by starting an email off with "Will you be able to…" and then there's no question that follows up with that in the email itself. You want to make sure that you're congruent and actually asking that full question there.

Another key thing with your emails is that you should include a set time whenever you would ideally like to have a conversation with the customer, or, alternatively, an easy way for them to schedule one with you. If it seems that they're wanting to have a conversation with you from their last email, and you're not able to reach them by phone, remember to include an easy way for them to schedule with you in the follow-up email.

I usually like to let people know that they are welcome to call me but that I am busy; it may be best if they shoot back two or three times that work for them in the next couple days for us to connect. Or, you can simply say: "go ahead and use the link below," and send your TimeTrade link and let them self-schedule a time. My ability to get hold of people has gone up tremendously once I started giving them the ability to schedule time with me right in the emails that I sent to them.

The other thing that you should be doing is paying very close attention to what you are sending to people by email on a regular basis. Then, you can start taking that text (whether it be completely emails or whether it be particular questions and answers) and putting it into template, so that you can cut and paste.

I see way too many people who may answer the same question two, three, a half a dozen or even a dozen times a day through email; and they type it out each and every time they send it. You need to find a way of saving yourself some time; templatize that stuff – this way, you can drop it off in an instant into your email. Using technology to automate parts of what you do will save you tremendous amount of time. Again, when you're spending your time brilliantly, you're going to have more time on the things that actually are really effective for you.

If you happen to be a Mac user, I highly recommend using a program called TextExpander. It allows you to assign short keyboard commands to automatically fill in entire pieces of text. You can type as little as two or three characters, and it will replace that with full-blown pieces of text that could be from a sentence long to multiple paragraphs with links and images and all that sort of stuff tied into it. It saves me a huge amount of time on a regular basis.

Bonus: emails that get results

Get a head start on sending emails that get results. Text **#EMAIL** to (847) 380-8117 and you'll receive my 25 top email templates. These are emails I have used to start lasting relationships with clients, generate millions of dollars of sales, and have saved me hundreds of hours. Don't reinvent the wheel... Start with these emails that have been proven to work again and again.

―――――――――――――――――――――――――

How do I create urgency in my prospect?

Another challenge that a lot of people end up having is getting deals to close as quickly as they'd like. This really boils down to making sure that you've instilled a good sense of urgency into the sales process... and there's a number of ways that you can do that.

One way is to insert an expiration date into your core offer. You want to make sure every time you're presenting a solution to a customer that you give a date when that offer would be over; and ideally, you should be coupling that with a reason why that it is ending. If you just say, "This is only good until Tuesday" or "This is only good until Wednesday" without any reason behind it, it's less likely for your prospect to believe that it's really a valid expiration date.

You want to make sure that you couple the expiration date with why it's ending then, and you can let them know that it can be tied to the fact that you're filling your schedule for next month's clients pretty quickly here. So to make sure that they get scheduled in time to have the project done, you need to know by Tuesday. Or, it could be that if there's a physical component to what it is you're offering, it could have to do with availability of getting the physical components together and delivered on time or ensuring that you still have something left in stock.

That's one of the things that you should be doing with every proposal you make in order to make sure that there's some urgency built around it. But the bottom line ends up being that it's very difficult for you to create urgency in your customer; indeed, the urgency really needs to come from them. The best way to do that is to make sure that during the course of the sales process, you are getting them to tell you how important this is and the timelines around it.

The first thing that I like to do when I'm talking to a prospect about a potential solution is just to simply ask them what their timeframe for wanting to solve this problem is; or better yet, the timeframe to get the result that you guys have talked about.

Thus, you simply ask them straight out, "By what date do you wanting to start having the extra hundred leads each month come into your business?" or "By when is it that you want to have the new shopping cart installed in order to make sure it's easier for your customers to complete their purchases?" Just ask them up-front what their timeline is. Once they give you a timeline, follow up by asking them why they need the result by then. Knowing their why is an important part of ensuring that the timeline is true, and not just something they thought of off the cuff. Having the why is also psychologically important that they express it along with the reasoning.

Once you've heard a timeline from them, and you've gone through determining exactly what it is that they're really looking for, the next thing that you want to do is have them tell you how urgent this is for them... and luckily, there's a great process for doing that. There are just a couple of quick questions that you can ask that get this framed really well, and it will tell you if it really is important to them or not. If it is important, it's going to get them talking about how important and specifically why; which will give you all the reasons you need to convince them that they should make a decision quickly.

You can do this right after you've gone through the process of finding out from them why it is that they're interested in your solution, what it means for them and what it's going to do for them. You can just simply ask them, "All right, so on a scale of 1 to 10, how important is it for you to..." and then fill in what it is that they said that they want to do. Again, it's just, "On a scale of 1 to 10, how important is it for you to..." and then whatever end result you guys are looking for.

When they give you an answer, what you want to do is say something along the lines of, "Great. Thanks so much for sharing that with me. It helps a lot. I'm curious about why you did not pick a lower number than…" and whatever number they said. They may tell you, "On a scale of 1 to 10, it's a 7" or "it's an 8 or 9." So, you say, "Great, thanks for sharing that. I'm curious why did you not pick a number lower than 8?" Then just be quiet and wait for their answer.

What comes next is them giving you all the reasons why it's very important to get it done soon and what their reason behind the urgency is. It's a really great way of pulling reasons from the customer; not only instilling their own sense of urgency, but also making sure that you've got a number of hot buttons that you can use later when it comes time to build your proposal, present your solution and then ultimately, try to close the deal.

The other thing that I'd like to do is leave some extra incentives on the table that I don't include up-front. This way, if they are teetering on the brink of a decision and you need to push them over the edge, you can use them a little bit later. Ideally, these should not be some sort of discount that you'll offer to them, but something additional that you can throw in, some additional work that you can do that you normally wouldn't have charged much more for anyway.

Or it may be a product that has a very low cost to you and that you can toss in along with the original deal. All you have to do is to let them know, "Hey, I've got a few of these left. If you are able to make a decision by Saturday or by the end of the month [whatever timeline it is that you guys have set up in your proposal] I can throw this in for you."

Sometimes, it's just that little added incentive which can add a little bit more emotional juice to the pot and help to instill some urgency later on.

As business owners you have a lot on your plate. Finding time to dedicate to selling is often a challenge. We are inundated with deadlines for client projects, existing customers who want our attention, vendors who want our attention, social media, and hundreds of mundane tasks that distract us from what really matters. The first thing that is important in getting more time to sell is to take a hard look at what tasks you are doing and decide, which things you are doing that ultimately don't create value for your clients or revenue for you and then stop doing those. Some things you can probably just abandon.

The first step to getting back more time, is to know where your time is already going. Take a moment and write down everything that you normally do during a day. Every task you can think of you should write down. Don't limit yourself just to work tasks, literally write down everything you can think of that you do. Then examine the list and determine which things you may be able to leverage to do smarter, better or faster. There are several ways you can get some of these things off your plate or done better and faster.

Technology

Technology is one way of doing this. We are lucky to be in business in a time where technology has become so friendly and prolific. Here are just a few of the great tools and apps that can help you get more work done faster. Here are just a couple of my favorites

Text Expander by Smile Software is one of my two favorite technology tools. Text Expander allows you to type more with less effort! It saves your fingers and expands short keyboard shortcuts and transforms them into your frequently-used text and pictures. Take your most used email templates and fill them in with just a couple clicks. Phrases you use frequently are dropped into documents and emails instantly. While this may seem like not a big deal and mundane, but it adds up. So far this year Text Expander has expanded over 14,602 short snippets for me saving me 2,389,017 characters typed. With my typing speed that has saved me 100 hours in the first 75% of 2014. That's over 12 full 8 hour work days that I've gotten back.

Jing by TechSmith is another great tool. Jing allows you to capture what you see on your computer screen and mark it up with text, arrows, and highlights. You can also select any window or region and record a short 30 second to 5 minute clip of what happens in that area, complete with recording audio so you can explain or narrate. It makes communicating with prospects, clients, and employees quicker, simpler and more focused. What you used to communicate in email you can now demonstrate instantly while being more clear.

Unroll.me is a free service that intercepts your emailed newsletters and promotions. Email can be a huge distraction during the day. Especially when you have subscribed to dozens (or 100s) of newsletters. Many of us have find ourselves checking email every time the new mail indicator goes off. Even if you don't read the newsletter when it comes in, just the act of stopping what you are doing and seeing what came takes you out of your flow and slows down what you were working on. Ideally I recommend you turn of your email program and alerts for much of the day, but if you can't or won't do that or for the times that you do have it open, unroll.me consolidates these emails into a daily digest.

Popclip by Pilot Moon is a handy little mac app that instantly performs over 100 actions on anything you highlight with 1 click. Search google, amazon or LinkedIn. Paste what you highlight capitalized, uppercased or lowercased in 2 clicks. Look up the text you higgling in the dictionary, translate it to another language, or automatically paste it to dozens of other apps. Tweet it, send it to Facebook, or create a calendar entry. Sometimes even little actions can seem to make your work easier.

Instant Customer and **Traffic Geyser** is the ultimate lead generation, capture and follow up tool. With it you can easily capture leads, follow up with them automatically and distribute content across the Internet.

———————————————————————

BONUS: For a complete list of my the 20 best technology tools that help you work smarter, faster and better, text **#TECH** to (847) 380-8117.

———————————————————————

Outsource

Another of my favorite ways to get more done is to outsource as much work that doesn't directly and immediately generate revenue, yet takes up valuable time. Turning mundane, simple tasks over to someone else to complete for you is a great way to free up time. Taking tasks off your list that don't excite you, or where you may not be at your best when you do them will help you get better work, by finding someone better than you to do them.

For myself I have a part time assistant who I assign many administrative tasks to. For example, I don't check or listen to my own voicemails. A couple times a day she checks my voicemail and adds each to a google spreadsheet summarizing who the call was from, their return phone number, their email, and what they wanted or needed. Assuming just 6 voicemails a day averaging 3 minutes that is saving me 20 minutes a day. Accounting for people who may be hard to understand, or talk too fast causing you to have to re-listen to the message I save over 2 hours each week. That's an extra day every month. Just by not listening to my messages. I'm able to prioritize and act on each email much quicker this way. That doesn't even take into consideration that some of the questions that people ask of me are things she is able to answer for me using templates we have set up. As I recognize patterns of common questions that don't need my expertise to answer I'll build templates or record answers that she sends on my behalf right when the question comes in. My customer gets what they needed (probably faster than if they had to wait for me to respond personally) and I have less on my to do list.

Other tasks can be outsourced intermittently to others for reasonable costs quickly and easily. On Fivver.com you can find you can find people who would love to do your Graphics & Design work, online marketing, complete writing & translation tasks for you, edit your videos, compose music for you, or do simple programming, technical or advertising tasks for you for just Five Bucks. You can use oDesk or People Per Hour to find people who will work on a contract basis for you to complete larger or more complex projects for you. FancyHands has people who will make calls for you to set appointments, find out which of the Apple Store's near you has the iPad model you want in stock, or cancel your Showtime subscription. Task Rabbit is a great service that has local people who will run errants for you. Need cleaning done, a handyman or help moving a couple items. TaskRabbit will get it done for you economically and quicker than you could do it yourself. The more that you get off your plate, the more time you can free up to focus on your business. For some tasks you may pay as little as $5, others you may even spend $40 or $50 / hour, but if it frees you up to close a deal that pays you $250/hour then it's more than worth it.

Record

My mentor Mike Koenigs teaches a brilliant marketing tool called the 10 x 10 x 4 formula as a great way to generate traffic, leads, conversion and sales. It's also a brilliant way to save time and provide outstanding service to your prospects and customers. It's one of the best ways of leveraging technology to make time bend to your needs. Using a slight tweak to his formulate you will easily create content that helps your clients and prospects while:

- Positions you as an expert
- Helps you get found
- Establishes credibility and trust with your prospects
- Makes you stand out from your competition
- Provides extra value to your customers
- Save tons of time from answering the same questions over and over

If you are like many of the coaches, consultants and business owners I've spoken to you probably get lots of the same questions repeatedly. Sometimes you'll find that answering these questions for your customers and prospects takes up your time, but does nothing to actually drive a sale closer to being closed. By all means when you are with a customer live one on one you should answer the questions that they have, but often you'll get emails or voicemails from customers asking these same questions. Here is a great way to get some of these basic questions less often.

To get started you'll need a computer, an inexpensive camera (the one in your iPhone or Android phone will work).

Here are the steps:

1. Write down the top ten frequently asked questions you get about your product or service. This should take you less than 30 minutes. You probably know them off the top of your head.

2. Write down the top ten questions that potential customers should be asking you. These are the important things that differentiate you from your competitors and that while you may not be asked as frequently as you like, but wish they would. Spend another 15 to 30 minutes on this.

3. Record 20 short videos responding to each question. Keep these videos short. The response should be 30 seconds to 2 minutes long each.

4. Record 4 or 5 short supplemental videos.

    - A Call to Action Video. You'll outsource having this attached to the end of each of your 20 videos. This is an offer that entices them to move from your video to a web site that you'll use to capture their name and email address.

    - A Get them All Video. Record a video of you asking them to enter their name and email to get all 20 videos. You'll put this on a video lead page where you offer to give them access to 20 videos answering all the top questions about your topic. Imagine if your prospects watched all these videos before scheduling a one on one call with you. They'll know the most important things about you, and know, like and trust you before you speak. You'll find them much more open when you begin asking powerful questions.

    - Thank you for Signing Up. Put this on the thank you

page that you send someone to when they fill in one of your forms.

- Buy My Stuff Video. This is where you'll give your viewers an offer to buy your product or service.

- Talk to me Video. In this video you'll offer to schedule a one on one consultation with the prospect. When they watch this video you'll give them your scheduling link. This way you'll convert someone who originally was asking 1 simple question into a pre-scheduled consultation (sales call), where they are already educated about all your best stuff and want to talk to you about how to apply your expertise or product to their situation.

You can use Instant Customer plus Traffic Geyser to submit these videos to the search engines and get hits to your website and new visitors. These videos will also be used to blow away your prospect with over-delivering when they contact you with a question. Here is what you'll do. When you get a voicemail or email from a prospect with one of the questions from your list, the first thing that you'll do is call them. This is a buying signal, and you should prioritize personal contact with them. That being said, you may recall that contact rates these days hovers as low as 10%. That means that this hot prospect you you won't reach 90% of the time that you call them.

When you call and get their voicemail leave a message saying you got their voicemail (or email) and wanted to answer their question. Let them know that you are sorry you missed them and that you recorded a short video for them answering their question and you'll send them a link to it. Then send them an email (make it a template) with a link to that particular video from your 10 x 10 x4 sequence. Also tell them in the email that you'd love to talk to them further about it and include a link to your scheduling system (like TimeTrade). Your prospect will be blown away at the lengths you went to answer their question. It's likely they will watch your other videos as well. The end result is that you cut down on phone tag, get a <u>scheduled</u> call with your prospect who is now even further educated on you and your products and services.

Recommended Reading

I can not stress enough how important it is to always be learning. To that end here is a small segment of my recommended studies for you. This is not my entire list of favorite sales books, but is a great start. I recommend you read as many of these as you can:

- Agile Selling by Jill Konrath

- Attitude 101 by John C. Maxwell

- Green Eggs and Ham by Dr Suess [one of the best sales books every written. If you have not read it recently, pick up a copy and read it today]

- How I Raised Myself from Failure to Success in Selling by Frank Bettger

- How to Master the Art of Selling by Tom Hopkins

- How to Win Friend & Influence People by Dale Carnegie

- Influence: The Psychology of Persuasion by Robert Cialdini

- It's Called Work for a Reason!: Your Success Is Your Own Damn Fault by Larry Winget

- Little Red Book of Selling by Jeffrey Gitomer

- Pitch Anything: An Innovative Method for Presenting,

Persuading, and Winning the Deal by Oren Klaff
- Sales 2.0 for Dummies by David Thomspson
- Secrets of Question Based Selling by Thomas Freese
- Selling the Invisible by Harry Beckwith
- Shift! by Craig Elias
- SNAP Selling by Jill Konrath
- SPIN Selling by Neil Rackman
- SPIN Selling Field-book by Neil Rackman
- The Closers by Ben Gay III
- The Closers by Ben Gay III
- The Definitive Book of Body Language by Barbara Pease
- The Game by Neil Strauss
- The Greatest Salesman in the World by Og Mandino
- The New Strategic Selling by Robert B Miller and Stephen E. Heiman
- The Psychology of Selling by Brian Tracy
- The Sales Bible: The Ultimate Sales Resource by Ben Gay III
- The Ultimate Sales Machine by Chet Homes
- To Sell is Human by Daniel Pink
- Unlimited Selling Power by Donald Moine
- What Great Salespeople Do by Michael Bosworth

- You Can't Teach a Kid to Ride a Bike at a Seminar by David Sandler
- Ziglar on Selling by Zig Ziglar

Bonus: Education that Gets You More Sales

To get access to my continually updated list of recommended educational resources text **#LEARN** to (847) 380-8117 and I'll send you a link to my updated Recommended Reading list.

---

www.ingramcontent.com/pod-product-compliance
Lightning Source LLC
Chambersburg PA
CBHW051548170526
45165CB00002B/933